SMOKED SALMON & HERB
CHOCOLATE ORANGE SOUFFLÉS
CELERIAC and PARSLEY SOUP with
BALLINDALLOCH MINCE and CHEESY POTATO PIE
ROUGH CHICKEN LIVER PÂTÉ
CHICKEN WRAPPED with GOAT'S CHEESE
and WARM TOMATO DRESSING
GRILLED RACK OF LAMB with PLUM SAUCE
FILLET of VENISON with OAT and HERB CRUST
FILLET of PORK with a BLACK GRAPE & CRÈME FRAÎCHE SAUCE
ABERDEEN ANGUS BEEF PATTIES in an ORANGE & CAMPARI SAUCE
BALLINDALLOCH CHICKEN
MALADE and a WHISKY CREAM SAUCE
PHEASANT NUGGETS
HIGHLAND BRULÉE
MEDALLIONS of LAMB with an ONION & FENNEL MARMALADE surrounded by WHISKY SAUCE
JUBILEE PHEASANT
ENSE ET ANIMO
TOUCH NOT THE CAT BUT A GLOVE

CHOUX RINGS with SMOKED HADDOCK & PRAWNS

EGG & SALMON PARCELS with a HOLLANDAISE & CUCUMBER SAUCE

BALLINDALLOCH BEEF TOURNEDOS with a WHISKY CREAM SAUCE

FRICASSÉE of PARTRIDGE BREAST served on FRIED BREAD

BALLINDALLOCH BEEF TOURNEDOS with a WHISKY CREAM SAUCE

MUSTARDY PHEASANT BREASTS

STEAMED CHOCOLATE PUDDINGS with VANILLA SAUCE

RACK of LAMB with a PARSLEY & BREADCRUMB TOPPING served with a MINT HOLLANDAISE SAUCE

PORK CHOPS with GORGONZOLA

FILLET of BEEF in a CREAM, MUSHROOM and WHISKY SAUCE

STEVE'S CHOCOLATE CHEESECAKE

COLLOPS of ROE-DEER EN CROUTE

COLD LEMON SOUFFLÉ sprinkled with ALMONDS

TWICE BAKED LEMON SOUFFLES with a creamy LEMON SAUCE

LEMON TART served with an ORANGE & KIWI SALAD

UPSIDE DOWN PEAR and GINGERBREAD PUDDING served with TOFFEE SAUCE

To Oliver

Live well

Laugh often

Love much

I LOVE FOOD

138 ravishing recipes from the Lady Laird of Ballindalloch Castle

Clare Macpherson-Grant Russell

BALLINDALLOCH CASTLE

one of Scotland's most romantic castles.

Set in the magnificent surroundings of the Spey Valley it is known as 'The Pearl of the North'. The much loved family home of the Macpherson-Grants, it is one of the very few privately-owned castles to have been lived in continuously by its original family.

I have had more fun writing this book than you can possibly imagine. Time flies by in the winter, with all the required concocting and tasting filling the long Scottish evenings. Experimenting with new recipes is enormous fun. The only penalty is the effect that it has had on my waistline!

Forget the battle of the bulge – indulge!

introduction

'I LOVE FOOD'

My great love of cooking really began when I returned to my family home in 1978. Being an only child, I was lucky enough to inherit Ballindalloch Castle from my father, Sir Ewan Macpherson-Grant Bt. I became the twenty-second generation of my family to live here and, most important, the first 'Lady Laird'! For me, my husband Oliver and all the family, it is first and foremost a much-cherished family home. However, as the owner of any great house will tell you, "inheriting is the easy part, hanging on to it is the difficult part".

Ballindalloch is one of Scotland's most romantic castles. Known as the 'Pearl of the North', it is set in the magnificent surroundings of the Spey valley – a perfect place for entertaining, with its numerous sporting and other outdoor pursuits for people to enjoy. Over recent years we have developed a hospitality business based around the Castle, so that it more than pays for its upkeep. We have enjoyed every minute of our houseparties and our lives have been enriched by our guests. We have entertained chief executives, Ambassadors, Prime Ministers, Royalty and Hollywood Stars over the years and have made many delightful friends worldwide. Looking back over our twenty-five years, we would not have changed the way that we have welcomed the houseparties. They have given us great joy and the Castle never feels happier than when it is filled to the brim with people.

The various financial strategies for the Ballindalloch Estate, put in place over past decades by my husband Oliver and I, look set to ensure its continued success as one of the great Scottish castles and estates. Recent initiatives have included a golf course and a windfarm. What is significant is that none of this is change for its own sake. It is the sympathetic development of a Highland estate in tune with modern times; it is the use of innovation and forward planning to perpetuate a unique part of the heritage of the Scottish nation.

To begin with, when taking in houseparties, I was both 'cook and bottlewasher'. Hence I had to learn at breakneck speed how to produce the best possible food in the least possible time, and so began my real interest in cooking. I have never had a cooking lesson in my life, and have learned by trial and error. I love food but I am not prepared to spend hours slaving over the cooker. For this 'domestic goddess' the motto is very definitely 'Taste, Ease and Speed'!

We have had the most enormous fun putting together my favourite recipes and then trying them all out. We think they are sensational but easy. Our houseparties have been our unwitting guinea pigs and they have been extremely complimentary. I have included recipes in memory of my relations, such as General James Grant, old friends, and interesting personalities like Rob Roy Macgregor. The Aberdeen Angus beef recipes reflect the fact that we have the oldest herd in the world. My great-grandfather started the herd in 1860 and every Aberdeen Angus steak that you eat today can be traced back to the Ballindalloch herd.

I have added the stunning Ballindalloch Rose Bavarois in honour of our beautiful rose, bred for us by Alec Cocker to commemorate the Castle's 450th anniversary. The new Golf Course, designed for us by Donald Steel, and our son Edward's 'Happy Cow' sweetened condensed milk are each acknowledged in the names of recipes. Guy, our elder son and my best critic, also concocted a wonderful pudding, and our daughter Lucy's Chocolate Crunch is an old winner. Apart from the recipes, I hope that you will enjoy the stunning photographs of the dishes by Simon Walton, and my 'doggie' recipes, and that they will give you some amusement! I couldn't resist also adding some of my favourite family photographs, poems and sayings which I hope you will also enjoy.

This book would never have come about without Guy, and the skills and enthusiasm in the Castle kitchen of Steve Murray, our marvellous chef, and our dear family cook, Mrs Betty Cameron. Oliver has been a marvellous 'taster', and my assistant, Fenella Corr, has been instrumental in getting our ideas and experiments into writing and then revising the numerous drafts. That the book is so beautifully designed is due to the marvellous flair of Nick McCann.

I do hope that you will enjoy reading and using this book as much as I have enjoyed writing it. I also hope that you will find our favourite recipes delectable and easy, and that your dogs enjoy the ones for them too!

'TASTE, EASE AND SPEED'!

Food is a vital part of one's life, and we enjoy it at least three times a day. Forget the battle of the bulge – indulge!

Clare Macpherson-Grant Russell
Laird of Ballindalloch.

THE FIRST CLASS LADY COOK

We own an ancient castle but so up to date inside,
And we decorate and furnish it with ever-loving pride,
But there's another asset that deserves a closer look,
For everything depends upon our FIRST CLASS LADY COOK.

Our black cattle are acknowledged to produce the finest meat,
The birds from off our grouse moors are considered quite a treat,
We've a famous salmon river and when we get a hook,
We bear the fish in triumph to our FIRST CLASS LADY COOK.

We'll ask our friends to share our gastronomical delights,
Indulging jaded palates and rechêrché appetites,
Enjoying creature comforts, shaded lights and cosy nook,
The sluicing, and the browsing by our FIRST CLASS LADY COOK.

But we've a solemn warning for the morally unsound,
And we'll tell them all quite firmly when they come the first time round,
That however much they're tempted by the dishes in this book,
They're not to pinch, in either way, our FIRST CLASS LADY COOK!

A 'thank you' note from Brian Madden - one of my favourite guests!

I have included a Weights and Measures Chart on page 236 and an Index on page 238

RECI

starters

mains

puds

teas

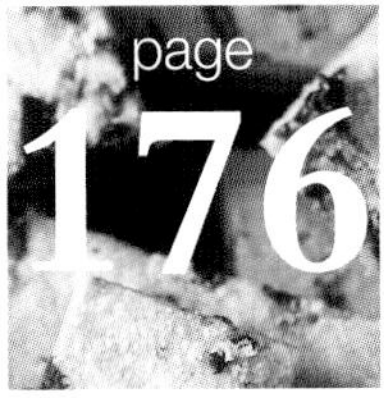

PES

starters
- FAVOURITE FIRST COURSES

starters - FAVOURITE FIRST COURSES

Early to Bed
Early to Rise
Fish all Day
Make up Lies

AVOCADOS & SCALLOPS

Simple style - melts in the mouth.

INGREDIENTS

2 tablespoons oil
8 ozs (225g) queen scallops, trimmed
Garlic (optional)
2 ripe avocados, halved, stoned and sliced
Juice and zest of 1 lime/lemon
1 tablespoon mayonnaise (home-made if possible)
1 tablespoon crème fraîche
2 rashers bacon, fried and diced
Bag of herb leaves for decoration

METHOD

Heat oil in pan and toss trimmed scallops in it for about 2 minutes till opaque. Remove and keep warm. Halve, peel and stone avocados. Slice lengthways and place in ear-dishes. Shred a little lettuce and make nest for scallops. Mix 1 tablespoon of mayonnaise and 1 tablespoon of crème fraîche in bowl with juice and zest of the lime. Season. Add scallops and mix well. Place scallops on bed of lettuce and sprinkle with warm bacon.

BROCCOLI & SMOKED HADDOCK SOUP

Lovely and creamy – the ingredients work so well together.

INGREDIENTS

1 lb (450g) broccoli
2 ozs (50g) butter
1 finely sliced onion
1 sprig of thyme
1 bay leaf
9 ozs (250g) natural smoked haddock fillet, skinned and diced
1½ pts (900ml) milk
Seasoning

METHOD

Cut broccoli into small florets. Melt butter, add broccoli, onion, thyme and bay leaf. Stir to coat vegetables and leave to sweat over very gentle heat for 10 minutes. Add haddock, milk and seasoning. Bring to boil and simmer, covered, for 10-15 minutes. Remove bay leaf and thyme, liquidise until smooth and flecked with green. Serve with crusty French bread.

CELERIAC & PARSLEY SOUP WITH CRUMBLED STILTON

I adore this soup. Celeriac is so tasty and the Stilton adds a sharp flavour.

INGREDIENTS

1 oz (25g) butter
1 tablespoon vegetable oil
2 large onions, finely chopped
1 lb 9 ozs (700g) celeriac
1½ pts (900ml) vegetable stock
1 pt (600ml) milk
1 bunch parsley
6 ozs (150g) crumbled Stilton
Few sprigs of thyme
1 carrot, chopped

METHOD

Melt butter and oil in large pan, add onions and carrot and gently fry till soft. Meanwhile, peel celeriac and cut into 1" (2.5cm) chunks. Add celeriac to pan, stir well and add stock and thyme. Bring to boil, stir and cover. Simmer for about 20 minutes till vegetables are tender. Place in processor and whizz. Return to pan, stir in milk. Season and reheat. Place in individual soup bowls, sprinkle each one with crumbled Stilton and parsley. Serve with Mrs D's Scottish Brown Bread.

serves 4

CRISPY PARMA HAM WITH AVOCADO & WARM TOMATO DRESSING

The perfect recipe for those who don't like standing on the scales!

INGREDIENTS

5 tablespoons olive oil
3 ozs (75g) Parma ham, roughly torn
2 large plum tomatoes, quartered, seeded and finely sliced
1 bunch fresh basil, chopped
Juice of 1 lemon
Bag mixed herb salad
1 large ripe avocado, peeled, stoned and sliced
Seasoning

METHOD

Heat tablespoon of olive oil in non-stick frying pan over high heat. Add half the Parma ham pieces, sprinkle with ground black pepper and fry for 1 minute till crisp. Set aside and fry the rest. Place on kitchen paper to soak up excess fat. Heat remaining olive oil and add tomatoes, basil and lemon juice. Warm gently for about 30 seconds. Arrange salad on 4 plates. Divide avocado slices between them. Sprinkle on crispy ham and drizzle with tomato and basil sauce. Serve with warm French bread.

serves: 6

EGGS BALLINDALLOCH

A superb Sunday supper dish.

INGREDIENTS

8 hard-boiled eggs, chopped
8 ozs (225g) large prawns
3 ozs (75g) grated cheese
½ pt (300ml) single cream
2 ozs (50g) butter
1 tablespoon chopped parsley and chives
1 teaspoon French mustard
Seasoning to taste

METHOD

Melt butter in saucepan. Add chopped eggs, prawns, parsley, chives, mustard, cream and seasoning to taste. Mix well over a low heat. Place in ovenproof dish. Sprinkle with grated cheese and dot with butter. Grill or bake till golden-brown. Serve with pasta and melba toast.

FIG & GOAT'S CHEESE SALAD

A doddle!

INGREDIENTS

8 slices of prosciutto ham
4 ripe figs
Bag of salad leaves
4 ozs (100g) soft goat's cheese

For the dressing:
3 tablespoons olive oil
1 tablespoons red wine vinegar
1 tablespoon runny honey
1 teaspoon fresh thyme leaves (freshly chopped)
Seasoning

METHOD

For the dressing, mix all ingredients together and season. Place 2 slices of prosciutto and 1 fig, quartered, on plate. Top with salad leaves, then crumble goat's cheese over and drizzle the dressing over the top. Serve with warm French bread.

wild thyme

FIGS, PARMA HAM & ROCKET WITH PARMESAN

A really lazy, lovely starter.

INGREDIENTS

4 really large ripe figs
8 slices of best Parma ham
A bag of rocket salad
5 ozs (125g) Parmesan cheese
Olive oil
Black pepper

METHOD

Place washed rocket on plates. Halve the figs and arrange with Parma ham. Crumble Parmesan into big lumps and sprinkle between plates. Drizzle with olive oil and grind over black pepper.

GOAT'S CHEESE & THYME SOUFFLÉS

To die for!

INGREDIENTS

4 eggs, separated
8 ozs (225g) soft goat's cheese, diced
4 ozs (100g) Parmesan cheese, finely grated
6 tablespoons double cream
1 large teaspoon finely chopped fresh thyme, plus extra leaves for decoration
Seasoning

METHOD

Whizz egg yolks in bowl till smooth. Add goat's cheese and whisk again. Stir in cream and chopped thyme. Season and fold in half the Parmesan cheese. Whisk egg whites in bowl with pinch of salt till stiff, then fold carefully into cheese mixture. Divide mixture between 4 greased ramekin dishes and sprinkle with remaining Parmesan. Place on hot baking tray and bake at 400°F/200°C/Gas 6 for about 10 minutes till risen and golden. Serve immediately with a herb salad.

Thyme on my side ~
time on my hands

Address to a Haggis -

Recited at every Burns' Supper celebrated around the poet's birthday on the 25th January. The closing stanza is said to have been composed by Burns 'off the cuff' during a dinner

But mark the Rustic, haggis-fed,
The trembling earth resounds his tread,
Clap in his walie nieve a blade.
He'll make it whissle;
An' legs an' arms, an' heads will sned,
Like taps o' thrissle.

Ye Pow'rs, wha mak mankind your care,
And dish them out their bill o' fare,
Auld Scotland wants nae skinking ware
That jaups in luggies:
But, If ye wish her gratefu' prayer,
Gie her a Haggis!

Meaning of unusual words in Burns' poem:

sned - trim
taps o thrissle - tops of thistle
skinking - watery
jaups - splashes
luggies - wooden bowl
with projecting
handles

THE NOBLE HAGGIS

What a pity that the haggis is often viewed with horror and humour. However, it has long been a traditional way of using up parts of the animal which otherwise might go to waste. It is a tasty, nutritious dish, with each cook creating his or her own recipe to get the flavour and texture (dry or moist) that suits them.

INGREDIENTS

Set of sheep's heart, lungs and liver (cleaned by a butcher)
One beef intestine
3 cups finely chopped suet
One cup medium ground oatmeal
Two medium onions, finely chopped
One cup beef stock
One teaspoon salt
½ teaspoon pepper
One teaspoon nutmeg
½ teaspoon mace

METHOD

Trim off any excess fat and sinew from the sheep's intestine and, if present, discard the windpipe. Place in a large pan, cover with water and bring to the boil. Reduce the heat and simmer for an hour or possibly longer to ensure that they are all tender. Drain and cool. The oatmeal can be warmed in an oven until it is thoroughly dried out. Finely chop the meat and combine in a large bowl with the suet, oatmeal, finely chopped onions, beef stock, salt, pepper, nutmeg and mace. Make sure the ingredients are mixed well. Stuff the meat and spices mixture into the beef bung which should be over half full. Then press out the air and tie the open ends tightly with string. Make sure that you leave room for the mixture to expand or else it may burst while cooking. If it looks as though it may do that, prick with a sharp needle to reduce the pressure. Place in a pot and cover with water. Bring to the boil and immediately reduce the heat and simmer, covered, for three hours. Avoid boiling vigorously to avoid bursting the skin. Serve hot with "champit tatties and bashit neeps" (mashed/creamed potato and turnip/swede). A little whisky can be poured over the haggis, Drambuie is even better! At Burns Suppers, the haggis is traditionally piped in and Burns' "Address to the Haggis" recited over it.

HAGGIS MUSHROOMS

An interesting mix of flavours.

INGREDIENTS

4 large field mushrooms
1 tin haggis
4 ozs (100g) grated Parmesan cheese

METHOD

Clean mushrooms and remove stalks.
Fill centres with haggis.
Sprinkle with Parmesan.
Bake at 400ºF/200ºC/Gas 6 for about 10 minutes. Serve individually on a bed of mixed salad, drizzled with a French dressing.

Field fungi at Ballindalloch

HAGGIS TARTLETS WITH RED ONION MARMALADE & A WHISKY CREAM SAUCE

For those dreaming of their Celtic roots!

INGREDIENTS

For the pastry:
4 ozs (100g) butter
6 ozs (150g) plain flour
1 teaspoon Parmesan Seasoning

Filling:
2 tins of haggis

For the red onion marmalade:
3 medium red onions, peeled and finely chopped
2 tablespoons olive oil
4 tablespoons red wine
1 tablespoon dark muscovado sugar
2 tablespoons cider vinegar
Parsley for decoration

Whisky sauce:
½ pt (300ml) double cream
Whisky to taste

METHOD

Place pastry ingredients in processor and mix until like fine breadcrumbs. Mould into 6 greased tartlet tins and put in fridge to cool. Bake at 350ºF/180ºC/Gas 4 for about 15-20 minutes. Keep warm.

For the red onion marmalade, sauté onions in oil till softened. Add vinegar, wine and sugar. Bring to boil and simmer for about 20 minutes till reduced and thick. Season and keep warm.

Warm double cream and add whisky.

Place haggis in pan and heat till piping hot. Spoon into warm tartlets, top with onion marmalade, sprinkle with parsley and serve with warm whisky sauce.

serves 6

PRAWN, EGG & AVOCADO MOUSSE

A very special combination.

INGREDIENTS

½ oz (11g) sachet gelatine
Juice and zest of 1 lemon
4 large eggs, hard-boiled, peeled and diced
6 ozs (150g) peeled prawns, roughly chopped
4 tablespoons Hellman's or home-made mayonnaise
4 tablespoons fresh dill, finely chopped
1 tablespoon Worcestershire sauce
1 large ripe avocado, halved, stoned, peeled and diced
½ pt (300ml) double cream
2 egg whites
Seasoning
Dill for garnish

METHOD

Lightly grease 6 small ramekins. Wrap a piece of buttered greaseproof paper around each dish, standing about 1" (2.5cm) above edge of ramekin. Secure firmly with tape. Place gelatine, lemon juice and 1 tablespoon hot water in bowl and place over pan of hot water. Stir until melted and clear. Cool slightly, and then mix in mayonnaise, zest of lemon, dill and a few drops of Worcestershire sauce. Mix chopped eggs, prawns and avocado in medium bowl. Stir in gelatine mixture, fold in whipped cream. Whisk egg whites till stiff and fold into mixture gently. Season to taste. Spoon into ramekins to just below top of paper. Chill for about 4 hours. Garnish with sprigs of dill and serve with melba toast.

MELTING MUSHROOMS

A winner every time!

INGREDIENTS

8 large field mushrooms
2 tablespoons olive oil
Juice of 1 lemon
1 tablespoon fresh breadcrumbs
4 ozs (100g) Dolcelatte or Gorgonzola cheese
2 tablespoons double cream
2 ozs (50g) freshly-grated Parmesan cheese
Seasoning and garlic to taste
2 tablespoons finely chopped parsley

METHOD

Clean mushrooms and remove stalks. Finely chop stalks and set aside. Place mushrooms on baking tray, stalk side up. Mix together olive oil, lemon juice, breadcrumbs, seasoning and garlic to taste. Fry chopped mushroom stalks in teaspoon of olive oil then add to breadcrumb mix. Spoon mixture into centre of mushrooms and place under hot grill for 5 minutes. Place Dolcelatte or Gorgonzola in small pan with cream and melt over gentle heat, stirring to combine. Put mushrooms in ear-dishes and spoon Dolcelatte mixture over mushrooms. Sprinkle with Parmesan and grill for 5 minutes till golden and bubbling. Serve sprinkled with parsley.

ROQUEFORT TART

A delight for a cheese-oholic!

INGREDIENTS

Pastry:
4 ozs (100g) butter
6 ozs (150g) plain flour
1 teaspoon Parmesan cheese

Filling:
8 ozs (225g) cream cheese (Philadelphia)
¼ pt (150ml) double cream
3 eggs, beaten
6 ozs (150g) Roquefort/Stilton cheese
Seasoning
Grated nutmeg
2 tablespoons fresh chives, finely chopped
Bag of herb salad

Walnut dressing:
3 tablespoons walnut oil
1 tablespoon vinegar
1 teaspoon runny honey
A few chopped walnuts
Seasoning

METHOD

Whizz pastry ingredients in processor till like fine breadcrumbs. Mould into greased 7" (17.5cm) flan dish. Cool in fridge. Place on hot tray and bake at 350°F/180°C/Gas 4 for 20-25 minutes. Cool.

For filling:
Meanwhile, place cream cheese in bowl and beat until soft. Beat in double cream and eggs. Crumble Roquefort/Stilton and fold in gently. Season with black pepper and nutmeg. Stir in chives. Pour filling into pastry case and bake at 375°F/190°C/Gas 5 for about 30-35 minutes till set and golden-brown. Meanwhile, make dressing by mixing all ingredients together. Slice and plate tart individually, serving with a herby side salad, drizzled with walnut dressing.

serves 8

ROUGH CHICKEN LIVER PÂTÉ

My favourite pâté – so simple to make.

INGREDIENTS

8 ozs (225g) chicken livers
4 rashers streaky bacon
(grilled)
2 finely chopped onions
8 prunes, stoned
5 ozs (125g) butter
Salt and pepper

METHOD

Fry onions and chicken livers in butter. Add stoned prunes, chopped grilled bacon and seasoning. Mash roughly with a fork and place in pâté dish. Leave in fridge to set for at least 2 hours. Cover with melted butter and cool. Serve with hot French bread.

serves 6

SALMON TERRINE

Looks really pretty and is very easy.

INGREDIENTS

5 ozs (125g) breadcrumbs
1 lb 5 ozs (600g) fresh salmon fillets
Seasoning
2 tablespoons wine
2 ozs (50g) butter
4 egg yolks
1 dessertspoon horseradish
Bay leaf
Pinch nutmeg
6 slices smoked salmon
2 avocados, halved, stoned and peeled
1 tub (200g) crème fraîche
1 dessertspoon horseradish
1 jar mock caviar

METHOD

Poach salmon fillets in wine with bay leaf and enough water to cover. Skin salmon and flake fish into processor. Add breadcrumbs, 1 dessertspoon horseradish, half the butter, the egg yolks and a pinch of nutmeg. Season, and whizz till smooth. Line a 1lb (450g) bread tin with buttered foil. Place 2-3 slices of smoked salmon at base of tin. Spoon over half of the salmon mixture. Place the halved avocados along the centre with stone cavity downwards. Place rest of mixture on top. Finish with 2 more slices of smoked salmon. Fold foil over top tightly. Place in a bain-marie (a roasting tin half filled with hot water) and bake at 300°F/150°C/Gas 2 for about 1 hour, till set. Remove from bain-marie. Cool and leave in fridge for several hours. Invert onto plate, peel away foil and serve sliced with crème fraîche with a spoonful of horseradish and black pepper added. Sprinkle with mock caviar and serve with herby bread.

serves 6-8

SMOKED HADDOCK & PARSLEY MOUSSE

Quick and can be made the night before.

INGREDIENTS

2 lbs (900g) smoked haddock
2 pts (1200ml) milk
1 onion
1 sachet of gelatine
6 tablespoons mayonnaise
¼ pt (150ml) fromage frais
Black pepper
3 tablespoons chopped parsley or cucumber curls for garnish
2 egg whites

METHOD

Place fish in large saucepan with milk and onion. Cook over moderate heat till soft. Cool. Take ¼ pt (150ml) of fish milk and place in small pan. Sprinkle in the gelatine and warm till dissolved. Flake the fish, removing all bones and skin, into large bowl. Add mayonnaise and fromage frais. Stir in cooled gelatine, season with ground pepper and sprinkle with parsley. Whisk egg whites till stiff, then fold into mixture gently and thoroughly. Place in glass serving bowl. Refrigerate for several hours. Decorate with parsley or cucumber curls.

SMOKED HADDOCK MOUSSELINES WITH A PRAWN & HOLLANDAISE SAUCE

The most popular starter of all – looks sensational, as if you have trained under the top chefs of the world.

INGREDIENTS

10 ozs (250g) smoked haddock
2 eggs, lightly beaten
Salt and pepper
Nutmeg
½ pt (300ml) double cream

METHOD

Skin and chop fish. Liquidise with salt, pepper and nutmeg. Blend in beaten eggs and put in fridge for a few hours. Place in liquidiser with cream and process. Butter cocotte dishes well and pour mixture into them. Stand in bain-marie (a baking tin half-filled with hot water) and bake at 375ºF/190ºC/Gas 5 for 30 minutes. Leave to stand for 2-3 minutes. Turn out and serve with prawn hollandaise.

Hollandaise with Prawns:
4 egg yolks
1 tablespoon water
2 tablespoons lemon juice
6 ozs(150g) melted butter
4 ozs (100g) large prawns
Salt and pepper

METHOD

Whisk egg yolks, water and lemon juice in a bowl over hot water. Pour in melted butter and whisk until thick. Add prawns and seasoning to taste.

P.S. If it curdles, add an ice cube and whisk like mad!

P.P.S. Can be made in advance and kept in a thermos.

serves 8

SMOKED HADDOCK ROULADE WITH MUSHROOMS

I love all smoked fish and this is a delicious combination.

INGREDIENTS

1½ lbs (700g) smoked haddock
1½ pts (900ml) milk and water mixed
1 onion, skinned
2 ozs (50g) butter
2 ozs (50g) plain flour
Pinch nutmeg
Seasoning
4 eggs, separated
2 ozs (50g) strong Cheddar cheese

For mushroom filling:
1 oz (25g) butter
1 oz (25g) flour
½ pt (300ml) milk
1 lb (450g) sliced mushrooms fried in a little butter
Seasoning

METHOD

Bring fish, milk, water and onion slowly to boil. Simmer for 5 minutes. Leave to cool. Strain and reserve liquid. Remove skin and bones from fish. Line a Swiss roll tin with non-stick baking parchment. Melt butter and add flour. Cook for 1 minute then add 1 pt (600ml) of reserved liquid gradually, whisking like mad to prevent lumps. Cool. Add seasoning and beat in egg yolks, one by one. Flake fish and stir into sauce. Whisk egg whites till stiff and fold into mixture. Sprinkle grated cheese onto baking paper and pour mixture on top. Smooth. Bake at 350ºF/180ºC/Gas 4 until firm to touch. While cooking make filling. Fry finely sliced mushrooms in butter. Make white sauce by placing butter, flour, milk and seasoning in pan over gentle heat. Whisk like mad till butter is melted and sauce is thick and creamy. Add mushrooms and keep warm. When roulade is cooked, place piece of non-stick parchment on table and turn roulade out onto it. Spread filling over and roll up. Ease roulade onto serving dish and sprinkle with grated cheese.

serves 8

SMOKED HADDOCK SOUFFLÉS WITH A CREAMY HERB SAUCE

Don't be daunted by the word 'soufflé' – these are a 'must'!

INGREDIENTS

1 lb 2 ozs (500g) undyed smoked haddock
½ pt (300ml) full-fat milk
2 ozs (50g) grated Parmesan
2 ozs (50g) butter
2 ozs (50g) plain flour
Pinch pepper and teaspoon English mustard
4 large eggs, separated

Creamy herb sauce:
1 pt (600ml) double cream
Bunch mixed herbs, finely chopped
Dash of lemon juice
Seasoning

METHOD

Place fish in pan with milk and bring slowly to boil. Cover and leave for 30 minutes, then drain over sieve, reserving liquid. Place butter, flour, mustard, pepper and fish milk in pan and whisk like mad till thickened. Stir in Parmesan and egg yolks, one at a time. Skin and flake fish into mixture, being careful to remove any bones. Whisk egg whites with pinch salt till stiff. Gently fold into mixture. Divide mixture between 8 buttered ramekins. Place on hot baking tray and bake at 400ºF/200ºC/Gas 6 for about 15-20 minutes, until they are puffed up and golden-brown.

Meanwhile, heat double cream and sprinkle herbs in with dash of lemon juice. When soufflés are ready, break open the top and spoon a little sauce into the middle, and sprinkle with parsley. Serve immediately.

THESE ARE MY MOUNTAINS

For fame and for fortune I wandered the earth
And now I've come back to the land of my birth
I've bought back my treasures but only to find
They're less than the pleasures I first left behind.

For these are my mountains and this is my glen
The braes of my childhood will know me again
No land's ever claimed me tho' far I did roam
For these are my mountains and I'm going home.

The burn by the road sings at my going by
The whaup averhead wings with welcoming cry
The loch where the scart flies at last I can see
It's here that my heart lies, it's here i'll be free.

For these are my mountains and this is my glen
The braes of my childhood will know me again
No land's ever claimed me tho' far I did roam
For these are my mountains and I'm going home.

Kind faces will meet me and welcome me in
And how they will greet me my ain kith and kin
The night round the ingle the old songs will be sung
At last I'll be hearing my ain mother tongue.

For these are my mountains and this is my glen
The braes of my childhood will know me again
No land's ever claimed me tho' far I did roam
For these are my mountains and I'm going home.

James Copeland

serves 6

SMOKED SALMON & HERB ROULADE

An interesting and unusual roulade.

INGREDIENTS

1 bag of herby salad
1 oz (25g) butter
1 oz (25g) plain flour
½ pt (300ml) warm milk
2 ozs (50g) grated fresh Parmesan
2 tablespoons chopped fresh parsley
2 tablespoons chopped fresh dill
¼ pt (150ml) crème fraîche
6 ozs (150g) smoked salmon, chopped
1 Boursin herb cheese
3 eggs, separated
Seasoning

METHOD

Place butter, flour and warm milk in saucepan and whisk like mad till thick. Stir in egg yolks, 1oz (25g) of Parmesan, chopped parsley, dill and seasoning. Whisk egg whites till stiff and fold into egg mixture. Pour onto a buttered 13" x 11" (33cm x 28cm) Swiss roll tin and bake at 350°F/180°C/Gas 4 for about 12-15 minutes. Leave covered with greaseproof paper for 15 minutes. Tip out onto greaseproof paper sprinkled with a little Parmesan. Mix together crème fraîche and Boursin cheese, spread over roulade. Sprinkle with smoked salmon pieces and roll up. Leave to firm up and cool. Sprinkle with rest of Parmesan and serve surrounded by a herby salad and tomatoes.

serves 6

SMOKED SALMON & DILL TARTLETS

These taste as good as they look.

INGREDIENTS

Pastry:
4 ozs (100g) butter
6 ozs (150g) plain flour
1 teaspoon grated Parmesan
Seasoning

Filling:
8 ozs (225g) smoked salmon
2 eggs
1 tablespoon chopped fresh dill, plus a few sprigs for decoration
½ pt (300ml) single cream
1 teaspoon horseradish sauce

METHOD

Place pastry ingredients in processor and mix until like fine breadcrumbs. Mould into 6 greased tartlet tins and put in fridge to cool. Bake at 350ºF/180ºC/Gas 4 for about 15-20 minutes. Cool.

For filling, cut salmon into strips and divide between tartlets. Whisk eggs and dill, mix in cream and horseradish sauce. Season. Pour into tartlets and bake at 350ºF/180ºC/Gas 4 for about 10-12 minutes till set.

Glenfeshie by William Beattie Brown 1831-1909

SPINACH & GOAT'S CHEESE ROULADE WITH A CREAMY PESTO SAUCE

These flavours are made to go together.

INGREDIENTS

½ pt (300ml) milk
2 ozs (50g) plain flour
6 ozs (150g) butter
4 ozs (100g) round of goat's cheese, chopped
2 ozs (50g) Parmesan cheese, freshly grated, plus extra for decoration
4 eggs, separated
8 ozs (225g) fresh shiitake mushrooms, sliced
10 ozs (275g) baby spinach leaves, washed
3 tablespoons crème fraîche
Seasoning

Pesto Cream Sauce:
1 pt (600ml) double cream
4 tablespoons pesto sauce

METHOD

Mix together milk, flour, 2 ozs (50g) butter in large saucepan. Bring to boil over low heat, whisking like mad till thick and creamy. Mix in goat's cheese and half the Parmesan. Cool. Beat in egg yolks. Season. Whisk egg whites till stiff. Gently fold whites into cheese mixture. Spread onto Swiss roll tin 12" x 8" (30cm x 20cm), lined with non-stick greaseproof paper. Bake at 375°F/190°C/Gas 5 for about 15 minutes till firm. Cool. Meanwhile, dust sheet of greaseproof paper with a little Parmesan cheese. Turn roulade out onto paper and gently roll up. Set aside.
Make filling: melt another 1 oz (25g) butter in pan. Add shiitake mushrooms and stir fry for 3 minutes. In separate pan place spinach with teaspoon of water and cook till spinach wilts. Drain well by pressing water out of spinach with potato masher. Add mushrooms and stir in crème fraîche. Season. Cool. Meanwhile, make pesto sauce. Place cream and 4 tablespoons pesto sauce in pan and bring to simmering point. Keep warm. Unroll roulade and spread with filling. Roll up again and place on buttered baking sheet. Brush with rest of butter and sprinkle liberally with Parmesan. Bake at 375°F/190°C/Gas 5 for 15 minutes till risen and golden. Serve immediately with the warm pesto sauce.

serves 6

SPINACH ROULADE FILLED WITH CHICKEN LIVER & MUSHROOM PÂTÉ

I love roulades, less nerve-racking than soufflés.

INGREDIENTS

1 lb (450g) creamed spinach (frozen is much the easiest)
½ oz (12g) butter
Salt and pepper
4 eggs, separated
1 tablespoon grated Cheddar cheese

Filling:
8 ozs (225g) chicken livers
2 finely chopped onions
5 ozs (125g) butter
Seasoning
4 ozs (100g) mushrooms
4 rashers bacon, chopped

P.S. If time is not on your side, buy some country pâté!

METHOD

Make pâté first. Fry onion and chicken livers in butter till just slightly pink in middle. Place in processor. Fry sliced mushrooms and add to chicken livers. Season. Whizz lightly. Fold in chopped bacon and lay aside. Line Swiss roll tin with non-stick baking paper. Heat spinach, add egg yolks and seasoning. Whisk egg whites and fold in gently. Spread mixture evenly onto tin and bake for 10 minutes at 400ºF/200ºC/Gas 6. When done, quickly turn roulade out onto non-stick baking paper sprinkled with Cheddar cheese. Peel off the paper that it was cooked on. Spread with pâté, tilt paper and roll roulade up. Sprinkle cheese over top. Serve warm on a bed of herby leaves.

Can be kept in a cool oven without spoiling – unlike soufflés!

serves 4

SMOKED SALMON BLINI CHEATS

Perfect for the modern working lady.

INGREDIENTS

4 thin small Scotch pancakes
4 ozs (100g) mascarpone
4 ozs (100g) smoked salmon
1 jar mock caviar
Bag salad leaves

METHOD

Spread pancakes thickly with mascarpone. Top with ruffled smoked salmon. To garnish, spoon caviar into the middle of pancake. Serve on a bed of salad leaves.

The nearby River Spey

serves 4

STILTON, GRAPE & WALNUT SALAD

Simplicity itself - wonderful when time is of the essence.

INGREDIENTS

3 ozs (75g) walnuts (or selection of nuts), toasted
Bag ready prepared lettuce
4 ozs (100g) Stilton, crumbled in large chunks
4 ozs (100g) seedless grapes

For the dressing:
2 tablespoons walnut oil
1 tablespoon sunflower oil
1 tablespoon sherry vinegar
1 tablespoon runny honey
Seasoning

METHOD

Toast nuts under grill or bake in oven at 325ºF/170ºC/Gas 3 for about 10 minutes. Arrange lettuce on plates then top with walnuts, cheese and grapes. Whisk dressing ingredients and drizzle over lettuce. Serve with Mrs D's Scottish Brown Bread.

serves 6

TOMATO, PARSLEY & GOAT'S CHEESE TART

Delicious for supper or for 'al fresco' meals.

INGREDIENTS

Pastry:
4 ozs (100g) butter
6 ozs (150g) plain flour
1 teaspoon Parmesan

Filling:
1 onion, peeled and finely sliced
1 tablespoon olive oil
12 ozs (350g) cherry tomatoes, halved
3 tablespoons chopped parsley
2 eggs
1 teaspoon Dijon mustard
½ pt (300ml) double cream
3 teaspoons Tabasco green pepper sauce
4 ozs (100g) roll of goat's cheese, sliced
1 garlic clove, crushed
Seasoning

METHOD

Whizz pastry ingredients in processor until like fine breadcrumbs. Mould into 7" (17.5cm) flan dish. Cool in fridge. Place on hot tray and bake at 350ºF/180ºC/Gas 4 for 20-25 minutes. Cool.

Filling:
Fry onion and garlic in oil for 4-5 minutes till soft. Mix with tomatoes and parsley in bowl. Spoon into pastry. Break eggs into bowl. Whisk with mustard, double cream, Tabasco and seasoning. Pour filling into pastry case, top with sliced goat's cheese and bake at 350ºF/180ºC/Gas 4 for about 30-35 minutes. Serve with a mushroom salad.

serves 4

TOMATO & COURGETTE TIMBALES WITH A PIQUANT TOMATO SAUCE

Looks extremely pretty and summery.

INGREDIENTS

2 courgettes
2 vine tomatoes, sliced
2 eggs + 2 egg yolks
1 tablespoon tomato ketchup
3 tablespoons double cream
2 teaspoons chopped fresh basil
Seasoning

Home-Made Tomato Sauce:
2 tablespoons olive oil
1 finely chopped onion
1 x 15 ozs (450g) tin of tomatoes
Sugar to taste
Teaspoon Lea & Perrins
Seasoning
A pinch of fresh basil/finely chopped parsley

METHOD

Cut courgettes into thin slices, place in covered bowl over pan of boiling water and steam for 4 minutes till 'al dente'. Layer courgettes and sliced tomatoes alternately in 4 buttered ramekins. Whisk together eggs, cream, tomato sauce, herbs and seasoning. Pour egg mixture over ramekins, dividing it evenly. Place in bain-marie (roasting tin half filled with hot water) and bake at 350ºF/180ºC/Gas 4 for 20-30 minutes till lightly set. Cool, then run knife around rims. Carefully turn out and serve accompanied with a piquant tomato sauce and some shredded lettuce and a mint leaf for garnish.

SAUCE

Fry finely chopped onion in oil. Add tomatoes and basil. Simmer for 10 minutes. Season. Add sugar and Lea & Perrins to taste. Liquidise. Serve warm or cold.

serves 6-8

TWICE BAKED CHEESE SOUFFLÉS WITH A CREAMY LEEK SAUCE

A delicious starter which never fails to impress – another real favourite.

INGREDIENTS

½ pt (300ml) milk
2 ozs (50g) butter
2 ozs (50g) flour
Pinch of dried mustard
6 ozs (150g) Cheddar cheese
4 eggs + 1 extra white
Salt and pepper

Leek sauce:
4 leeks
½ pt (300ml) double cream
1 oz (25g) butter
4 ozs (100g) grated fresh Parmesan
Nutmeg

METHOD

Melt butter, flour, mustard and milk slowly together, whisking like mad till it comes to boil. Add grated cheddar cheese and seasoning. Separate eggs and add egg yolks to sauce. Whisk all whites and fold into cheese mixture. Spoon into cocotte dishes, filling almost to the top. Stand in bain-marie (a baking tin half-filled with hot water) and bake for 15 minutes at 350ºF/180ºC/Gas 4. Cool and leave in cocottes for at least 6 hours.

Twenty minutes before dinner, butter a shallow ovenproof dish. Run a knife round the soufflés to loosen and turn out onto dish. Wash and chop leeks finely. Melt butter in pan, add leeks and fry over low heat till soft. Pour in cream, grated nutmeg and seasoning. Heat to boiling point. Pour around soufflés. Sprinkle with Parmesan and bake at 350ºF/180ºC/Gas 4 for 10 minutes. Serve immediately.

serves 4

HOT AVOCADOS WITH PRAWNS & BACON

A rather intriguing and unusual mixture.

INGREDIENTS

2 avocados, halved and stoned
8 slices bacon
4 tablespoons Hellmann's mayonnaise
1 small pkt 4 ozs (100g) prawns
4 tablespoons grated Cheddar cheese

METHOD

Fry bacon and chop. Scoop out avocados, dice and mix with Hellmann's mayonnaise, bacon and prawns. Place back in avocados, sprinkle with cheese and bake at 400ºF/200ºC/Gas 6 for 10 minutes.

P.S. If you serve fish as the main course you can swap prawns for gently fried mushrooms.

I love cooking with Scotch - I even put it in my recipes . . .

GLENFIDDICH ~ from a dream to a dram-
the only distillery in the Highlands to farm its own barley.

BALLINDALLOCH & GLENFIDDICH

A strong connection exists between our family and the 'Grants of Glenfiddich'. After the bloody Battle of Culloden, fought on 16th April 1746, one of the fleeing Jacobites, Alexander Grant, William's ancestor, sought succour at his namesake's, Alexander Grant, the Laird of Ballindalloch. His appeal was granted, and the Laird found him a vacant croft called Gightcot, far up on nearby Ben Rinnes. There he could be hidden from The Duke of Cumberland's prying Dragoons scouring the area requisitioning food for the army.

Images courtesy of Glenfiddich

William Grant started life as a herd-boy guarding the Duke of Fife's cattle on the hillsides in Speyside. With his wife Elizabeth by his side and his two daughters and seven sons, he rose to become the founder of what was to become William Grant & Sons, the famous Scotch whisky distillery. After 20 years of saving - the Scottish are good at that! - he realised his dream of creating "the best dram in the valley". With second-hand equipment, some land acquired on Speyside, and the services of one stonemason, he and his family built the Glenfiddich Distillery with their bare hands. And on Christmas Day 1887, William Grant and Sons' Pure Malt Whisky first ran from the stills, with the entire project costing a mere £800. Encouraged by his success, several other distilleries sprang up in the area but, not to be outdone, Grant decided to expand and acquired more land and water rights. Then, like an implausible Hollywood plot line, he acquired his master's castle of Balvenie, which he converted to his second distillery!
A Scottish fairy-tale come true if ever there was one.

serves 6-8

WHISKY TERRINE

A Scottish touch to chicken liver pâté.

INGREDIENTS

4 ozs (100g) butter
1 finely chopped onion
8 ozs (225g) chicken livers
8 ozs (225g) cream cheese
Seasoning
1 tablespoon Glenfiddich whisky
4 rashers grilled bacon
1 pkt oatcakes
Cranberry sauce

Swords at the ready in the old watch tower!

METHOD

Melt butter and fry onion till transparent. Add chicken livers (cut away any veins) and fry till just pink in the middle. Place in liquidiser with cream cheese and process.
Add seasoning and whisky to taste.
Place in pâté dish and fold in finely chopped grilled bacon. Cool.
If wished, melt some butter and pour over top of pâté. Chill and serve with oatcakes and cranberry sauce.

serves 4

BALLINDALLOCH HAGGIS MOUSSELINES WITH A WHISKY, CREAM & ONION SAUCE

Enhances the haggis!

INGREDIENTS

8 ozs (225g) haggis
6 ozs (150g) turnip
6 ozs (150g) creamed potatoes
Seasoning
Finely chopped parsley and chives for decoration

For Sauce:
1 finely sliced onion
1 generous glass Glenfiddich whisky
½ pt (300ml) double cream

For chef:
1 small glass whisky

METHOD

Cook turnip and mash with a little butter and seasoning. Cook potatoes and mash well (no lumps) with a little butter and seasoning. Cook haggis by wrapping in foil and placing in oven 350ºF/180ºC/Gas 4 for about 45 minutes. Assemble mousselines by layering turnip, haggis and lastly creamed potato into buttered ramekins. Place ramekins in bain marie (roasting tin half filled with boiling water) and bake at 350ºF/180ºC/Gas 4 for about 20-25 minutes. Meanwhile, make whisky sauce. Heat whisky in pan, take off heat and ignite. Pour in double cream and finely chopped onion and heat till boiling point. Keep warm. To serve, take mousselines out of oven, run knife round edge of them and invert onto plate. Drizzle with whisky sauce and sprinkle with finely chopped parsley and chives.

mains

- FAVOURITE MAIN COURSES

mains

mains - FAVOURITE MAIN COURSES

serves 2

BALLINDALLOCH BEEF TOURNEDOS WITH A WHISKY CREAM SAUCE

A great treat.

INGREDIENTS

2 Aberdeen Angus fillet steaks about 1" (2.5cm) thick
2 rounds of fried bread
2 ozs (50g) butter
1 finely chopped onion
4 ozs (100g) sliced mushrooms
¼ pt (150ml) cream
1 tablespoon whisky
2 teaspoons chopped parsley
2 ozs (50g) pâté

METHOD

Melt butter in pan and cook steaks until done as desired. Remove from pan and keep warm. Fry onion and mushrooms in pan with butter. Add whisky, cream, chopped parsley and seasoning. Simmer for a few minutes. Spread fried bread round with pâté. Place beef on round and serve whisky sauce separately.

serves 6-8

ABERDEEN ANGUS BEEF PATTIES IN AN ORANGE & CAMPARI SAUCE

An interesting and unusual combination.

INGREDIENTS

3 slices wholemeal bread (made into coarse breadcrumbs)
½ pt (300ml) milk
1 lb 5 ozs (575g) Aberdeen Angus sirloin steak (minced)
1 egg, lightly beaten
1 bunch of thyme, finely chopped
Zest and juice of 3 oranges
Seasoning
Flour for dusting
2 tablespoons olive oil
2 ozs (50g) sultanas
2 fl ozs (60ml) Campari

METHOD

In large bowl combine breadcrumbs, milk, beef, egg, thyme, seasoning and orange zest. Mix well until the mixture holds together. Form into rounds the size of an egg and flatten slightly. Dust with flour. Heat oil in pan and fry patties for about 5 minutes on both sides. Add the orange juice, sultanas and Campari and simmer gently for 12 minutes, turning the patties occasionally in the sauce. Serve with pasta and salad.

Ballindalloch 'Ericas', 1884, by David George Steell

CHICKEN FILLED WITH GOAT'S CHEESE

Perfect for the career lady whose vocabulary doesn't include 'time'.

INGREDIENTS

2 chicken breasts
1 oz (25g) goat's cheese
2 rashers rindless streaky bacon
Fresh herbs
Seasoning
1 tablespoon olive oil

METHOD

Slice chicken breasts lengthways and stuff with 1 oz (25g) goat's cheese. Wrap each breast in bacon. Place breasts on bed of herbs in ovenproof dish. Spoon over 1 tablespoon of olive oil and roast at 400ºF/200ºC/Gas 6 for about 30 minutes, until bacon is crispy. Serve with new potatoes and a mixed salad.

'what will be, will be' . . .

The Russell Coat of Arms surmounted by a goat!

serves 6-8

BALLINDALLOCH MINCE AND CHEESY POTATO PIE

This has to go in any Castle cook book. For those who have never cooked it – this recipe will be loved by one and all.

INGREDIENTS

1 lb (450g) minced Scotch beef
1 onion, chopped
2 tablespoons oil
Worcestershire and tomato sauces to taste
Seasoning
1 tablespoon plain flour
½ pt (300ml) beef stock
Gravy browning (optional)
1 lb (450g) lightly boiled potatoes

Cheese sauce:
1 oz (25g) butter
1 oz (25g) flour
½ pt (300ml) milk
2 ozs (50g) grated strong cheese
1 egg yolk
Seasoning

METHOD

Gently fry onion in oil. Sprinkle with flour and allow to colour. Add mince and cook over gentle heat for 5 minutes. Add stock, sauces and seasoning to taste. Simmer, stirring occasionally, for 20 minutes. Pour into fireproof dish. Cool. Cover with cheese sauce and then a layer of sliced potatoes. Sprinkle with grated cheese and place in hot oven 350°F/180°C/Gas 4 for 15 minutes.

METHOD

Place butter, flour and milk in pan and whisk madly until thick. Add egg yolk and cheese.

BALLINDALLOCH CHICKEN

When my brain freezes and I cannot think of another meal ~ I come back to this ~ my old favourite!

INGREDIENTS

8 chicken breasts
1 large onion, finely chopped
1 pt (600ml) cream
4 tablespoons tomato purée
8 slices ham
8 dessertspoons grated cheese

OLIVER AND I ON OUR SILVER WEDDING DAY 16TH SEPTEMBER 1992

METHOD

Fry chicken breasts gently in butter on both sides. Place in a flat dish and cover with a slice of ham. Fry onion in butter and place on top of chicken and ham. Then sprinkle thickly with grated cheese. Pour tomato purée into pan with juices, fold in cream and season. Heat and pour over chicken. Place in moderate oven 350°F/180°C/Gas 4 for 20 minutes. Serve with wild rice.

COLLOPS OF ROE DEER EN CROÛTE

Should melt in the mouth, if you have good, young roe deer.

INGREDIENTS

1 loin of roe deer
1 large onion
8 ozs (225g) mushrooms
1 lb (450g) puff pastry

Sauce:
2 tablespoons redcurrant jelly
1 tablespoon Worcestershire sauce
2 ozs (50g) butter
Rind and juice of 1 orange
1 tablespoon parsley
4 tablespoons port or red wine
Salt and pepper

METHOD

Slice loin into 1" (2.5cm) collops. Fry in butter quickly and seal in juices. Cool. Chop onion and mushrooms finely and fry lightly in butter. Cool. Roll out pastry and cut into circles big enough to cover collops. Place collop in middle of circle, top with onions and mushrooms and wrap up like a parcel. Bake at 375ºF/190ºC/Gas 5 for 10-15 minutes. Serve with a port sauce.

Port Sauce:

Melt butter and add rest of ingredients. Simmer for 5 minutes. Season and if too strong add a little stock or water.

CHOUX RINGS WITH SMOKED HADDOCK & PRAWNS

A perfect lunch dish.

INGREDIENTS

Choux Pastry:

3 ozs (75g) butter,
plus extra for greasing
7 fl ozs (200ml) water
4 ozs (100g) plain flour
3 eggs, lightly beaten
2 ozs (50g) mature Cheddar, grated

Filling:

12 ozs (350g) smoked haddock fillet, boned, skinned and cut into strips
½ pt (300ml) full cream milk
1 oz (25g) butter
1 oz (25g) flour
8 ozs (225g) bag of king prawns
2 ozs (50g) mature Cheddar,grated
1 tablespoon chopped parsley
Seasoning

METHOD

Melt butter in water in a pan and bring to boil. Quickly add flour altogether. Stir until paste is smooth and forms a ball. Remove from heat, cool slightly then beat in eggs gradually. Stir in cheese. Spoon mixture onto greased baking sheet to make four rings 4" (10cm). Bake at 425ºF/220ºC /Gas 7 for about 15 minutes until puffed and golden. Meanwhile, make filling. Poach skinned haddock in pan with the milk over gentle heat for about 3 minutes. Drain and reserve milk. Keep warm. Melt butter, add flour and reserved milk and whisk like mad until sauce thickens. Add cheese and seasoning. Fold in flaked fish and roughly chopped prawns. Remove choux rings and place on serving plates. Fill with fish mixture. Sprinkle with parsley and serve with a tomato salad.

EGG & SALMON PARCELS WITH A HOLLANDAISE & CUCUMBER SAUCE

Well worth the effort – utterly delicious.

INGREDIENTS

3 ozs (75g) long grain rice
½ pt (300ml) fish stock
12 ozs (350g) fillets of salmon
1 tablespoon fresh dill, chopped
2 teaspoons curry powder
6 small eggs (medium-boiled, peeled and cooled)
15 ozs (425g) puff pastry
Juice of ½ lemon
1 small egg, beaten
Seasoning

Hollandaise & Cucumber Sauce:
4 egg yolks
1 tablespoon water
2 tablespoons lemon juice
6 ozs (150g) melted butter
½ cucumber, peeled and diced
Seasoning

METHOD

Cook rice in fish stock. Drain and cool. Place salmon in large saucepan and cover with cold water. Gently heat till simmering point and poach for 8-10 minutes till flaky. Cool. Remove bones and skin and flake fish into rice. Add lemon juice, curry powder, herbs and seasoning. Mix well. Roll out pastry into 6 x 6" (15cm) squares. Brush edges with beaten egg. Place spoonful of rice and fish mixture into middle of each square. Push eggs into centre and top with a little more of rice and fish mixture. Pull over pastry corners to middle to form square parcel, pressing joins together firmly to seal. Brush parcels with more beaten egg. Place on baking sheet and bake at 425°F/220°C/Gas 7 for about 20 minutes. Reduce oven to 375°F/190°C/Gas 5 and cook for further 10 minutes. Meanwhile, make sauce. Whisk egg yolks, water and lemon juice in bowl over hot water. Pour in melted butter and whisk till thick. Season. Fold in diced cucumber. Serve parcels accompanied with warm hollandaise and cucumber sauce.

'Ebonite' by David George Steell 1856-1930

FILLET OF ABERDEEN ANGUS BEEF IN A CREAM, MUSHROOM & CRAGGANMORE WHISKY SAUCE

Aberdeen Angus is **The Best**. The pedigree herd was started by my great-grandfather, Sir George Macpherson-Grant of Ballindalloch, in 1860. It is now the oldest herd in existence. Interestingly, Sir George, with his friend, John Smith, founded the Cragganmore Distillery.

INGREDIENTS

1 fillet of beef
(Aberdeen Angus)
8 ozs (225g) mushrooms
¾ pt (450ml) cream
2 onions, finely chopped
6 baked field mushrooms
for garnish

Cragganmore whisky to taste

METHOD

Tie fillet with fine string to keep shape and roast (10 minutes per lb) in oven 400ºF/200ºC/ Gas 6 dotted with butter and seasoning. Take it out, untie string and keep warm. Meanwhile, fry onions and mushrooms in pan with butter. Then add whisky to taste, double cream and seasoning. Simmer for a few minutes and pour over sliced fillet. Garnish with a few baked field mushrooms down the centre. Serve with brown rice and purée of carrot and parsnip.

serves 6

CRUSTY LAMB WITH MANGOES & WALNUTS

Sensational - melts in the mouth.

INGREDIENTS

2 fillets of Scottish lamb – about 7 ozs (175g) each
6 ozs (150g) finely chopped mushrooms
8 ozs (225g) coarse country pâté
2-3 tablespoons olive oil
1 tin mangoes (strained and chopped) plus extra for decoration
1 small pkt chopped walnuts/pecans
2 x 13 ozs (375g) pkts of ready-rolled puff pastry
8 ozs (225g) large spinach leaves
1 large egg, beaten
1 garlic clove, finely chopped
Seasoning

METHOD

Heat 2 tablespoons olive oil in frying pan. Sear lamb fillets all over till browned. Remove from pan and set aside. Fry mushrooms and garlic lightly. Remove from pan with slotted spoon and set aside. Mix together pâté, mushrooms, garlic, chopped mangoes and walnuts. Season. Wash spinach leaves and place in saucepan. Cook gently till wilted. Squeeze water out well. Cool. Place ready-rolled pieces of puff pastry on board. Lay spinach leaves on top. Spread pâté mixture over spinach, then place fillets of lamb on each and fold into two neat parcels. Brush with beaten egg and place on baking tray. Rest in fridge for 10 minutes, then bake at 400°F/200°C/ Gas 6 for 20-25 minutes till pastry is crusty and golden. Serve sliced thickly with some warmed slices of mango on the side.

FILLET OF PORK WITH A BLACK GRAPE & CRÈME FRAÎCHE SAUCE

Tender and succulent.

INGREDIENTS

1 lb (450g) fillet of pork
2 tablespoons olive oil
Seasoning
2 teaspoons peppercorns, lightly crushed
2 tablespoons flour
3-4 tablespoons red wine vinegar
1 x 8 ozs (200g) pot crème fraîche
Chopped parsley for decoration
Bunch of black grapes

METHOD

Slice pork into about 8 pieces about 1" (2.5cm) thick. Heat oil in a frying pan. Place flour in bowl and season. Add pork pieces and dust off excess. Place in frying pan and cook for about 3-4 minutes on each side. Remove from pan using a slotted spoon and keep warm. Add red wine vinegar, grapes and crushed peppercorns to pan and swirl about. Take off heat and stir in crème fraîche and chopped parsley. Return pork to pan and spoon over the sauce. Re-heat for a few minutes (DO NOT BOIL). Season. Serve with ribbons of pasta and asparagus.

FILLET OF VENISON WITH A THYME & BLUEBERRY SAUCE

Full of flavours from the Scottish mountains.

INGREDIENTS

1 lb (450g) fillet of venison
A few leaves of fresh thyme, finely chopped
2 tablespoons oil
4 shallots, peeled and finely sliced
1 clove of garlic, peeled and finely sliced
1 tablespoon redcurrant jelly
1 glass of red wine
8 ozs (225g) fresh blueberries or blackberries
2 knobs of butter
Seasoning

METHOD

Slice venison into 1" (2.5cm) discs. Heat oil in frying pan and fry each slice of meat for about 2-3 minutes till browned but still pink inside. Remove from pan with slotted spoon and keep warm. Place shallots, finely chopped thyme and garlic in pan and fry gently for 2-3 minutes till translucent. Add wine and redcurrant jelly and reduce by half.
Mix in blueberries and simmer for a few minutes. Add two small knobs of butter, leave to melt, and season.
Serve venison plated on a bed of creamed potatoes/celeriac or green vegetables with blueberry sauce drizzled over top.

BALLINDALLOCH VENISON CASSEROLE WITH APRICOTS & CHESTNUTS

The sweet and sour taste is perfect.

INGREDIENTS

2 lbs (900g) venison or roe deer cut into 1" (2.5cm) cubes
3-4 tablespoons sunflower oil
2 onions, skinned and finely sliced
1½ pts (900ml) game stock
¼ pt (150ml) port or red wine
1 pkt dried apricots (chopped)
1 x 15ozs (400g) tin whole chestnuts
1 tablespoon redcurrant jelly
Seasoning

METHOD

Toss cubed venison in two tablespoons seasoned flour. Heat oil in pan and fry meat till brown.
Take out of pan and leave. Add sliced onions to pan and cook till soft.
Replace meat into pan with onions, stir in stock, redcurrant jelly, wine, chestnuts and dried apricots.
Stir till boiling point, then place in covered casserole and cook at 350ºF/180ºC/Gas 4 for 1-1½ hours.
Serve with mashed potatoes and purée of turnip.

serves 4

FILLET OF VENISON WITH OAT AND HERB CRUST

A Scottish dish with great texture.

INGREDIENTS

1 oz (25g) butter
3 tablespoons olive oil
2-3lb loin of venison
Seasoning
4 ozs (100g) medium pinhead oatmeal
Finely chopped parsley and thyme

METHOD

Heat butter and 1 tablespoon oil in roasting tin on hob until hot. Season venison well and brown all over for 4-5 minutes. Remove from pan and cool for 5-10 minutes. Mix together oatmeal, herbs, oil and lots of salt and pepper and press all over the meat. Return to roasting tin and roast at 400ºF/200ºC/Gas 6 for 15-20 minutes. Serve sliced with cranberry sauce, accompanied by potato dauphinois and broccoli florets.

serves 4 - allow 1 whole grouse per person

mains

ROAST BALLINDALLOCH GROUSE

This was my mother's grouse recipe –
it had to be included as we live in the heart of the Highlands, surrounded by grouse moor.

INGREDIENTS

4 grouse (plucked and drawn by the butcher – a nightmare doing it yourself!)
4 rashers rindless streaky bacon
2 ozs (50g) butter
Seasoning
4 pieces fried bread
Country pâté (home-made or bought)
Cranberry sauce

METHOD

Place dot of butter inside each bird. Cover with bacon and place in roasting pan. Season and dot with rest of butter. Roast at 375°F/190°C/Gas 5 for about 35 minutes, basting once or twice during cooking. Meanwhile, make fried bread and spread with pâté. Place birds on top and accompany with gravy, bread sauce, game chips and cranberry sauce.

GRILLED RACK OF LAMB WITH PLUM SAUCE

Stylish and different.

INGREDIENTS

1 x 500g punnet of plums (halved and stones removed)
6 extra plums for decoration
1 small red chilli (finely chopped)
2 tablespoons sugar
1½ teaspoons red wine vinegar
2 teaspoons lime juice
1 tablespoon redcurrant jelly
1 tablespoon honey
4 racks of lamb with approx. 3 chops in each (12 in total)
Seasoning
Fresh thyme to garnish

METHOD

Place plums, honey, chilli, sugar, redcurrant jelly, vinegar, lime juice and a tablespoon of water in small pan. Cook gently for about 20 minutes, until reduced. Remove from heat and strain. Brush the racks of lamb with glaze. Wrap ends of bones with foil and roast at 400°F/200°C/Gas 6 for about 25 minutes, brushing the lamb with glaze several times. Pour rest of sauce into small pan, add sliced, halved and stoned plums. Warm and serve with lamb. Accompany with rosti potatoes and spinach gratin.

JUBILEE PHEASANT

A brilliant recipe for those pheasants that look at you every time you open the deep freeze!

INGREDIENTS

6 pheasant breasts
12 ozs (350g) mayonnaise
1 tablespoon curry paste
¼ teaspoon ground ginger
1 tablespoon sultanas
6 ozs (150g) dried apricots, chopped
2 tablespoons chopped walnuts, plus a few to decorate
1 tablespoon mango chutney
Seasoning
Chopped parsley for decoration

The gamekeepers at Ballindalloch in the late 19th century

METHOD

Cook pheasant breasts, dotted with butter, in tin foil for 15-20 minutes at 350°F/180°C/Gas 4. Cool. Cut into small chunks. Combine mayonnaise with curry paste and ground ginger. Add all remaining ingredients. Fold in chunks of pheasant. Serve on large platter sprinkled with walnuts and parsley. Accompany with a rice salad.

MUSTARDY PHEASANT BREASTS

Homely, rustic flavour.

INGREDIENTS

2 pheasant breasts
3 ozs (75g) butter
4 teaspoons French mustard
1 tablespoon white wine vinegar
1 dessertspoon tarragon vinegar
2 tablespoons double cream
Cayenne pepper
Seasoning

METHOD

Place pheasant breasts on foil and dot with 1 oz (25g) of butter. Season and wrap in foil. Bake at 400°F/200°C/Gas 6 for about 15/20 minutes. Meanwhile make sauce by melting remaining butter in a bowl sitting in boiling water. Stir in mustard, then wine vinegar and tarragon vinegar. Cook for eight minutes, then add cream and seasoning. Place pheasant breasts in a serving dish and pour over the sauce. Sprinkle with cayenne pepper and serve with couscous and mange-touts.

The gamekeepers at Ballindalloch in the early 21st century

Good shots never grow old - they just pick up less birds

serves 4

LOIN OF LAMB WITH AN ONION & FENNEL MARMALADE SURROUNDED BY WHISKY SAUCE

Dead easy and looks amazing.

INGREDIENTS

2 red onions, finely sliced
2ozs (50g) butter + another
1 oz (25g) diced
1 tablespoon sugar
1 loin of lamb
2 courgettes
Rosemary
Seasoning
1 head of fennel, finely sliced

For Whisky Sauce:
1 tablespoon Ballindalloch
Castle malt whisky
½ pt (300ml) double cream
Seasoning
Chopped parsley

METHOD

Sauté red onion and fennel in 1 oz (25g) of butter, over a low heat until soft. Add sugar and cook for one minute. Remove and keep warm. Slice loin diagonally. Flatten slightly and sprinkle with rosemary. Season. Melt rest of butter in pan and fry the slices of lamb for one minute on each side. Remove and keep warm. Quick fry the courgettes until hot and then slice into thin strips. Place slices of lamb on plate and accompany with courgettes and the onion and fennel marmalade, surrounded with a whisky sauce.

METHOD

Heat cream until boiling, add whisky and season. Sprinkle in parsley.

serves 4

PHEASANT NUGGETS

Utterly delicious and a wonderful way of using up pheasants.

INGREDIENTS

5 pheasant breasts, cut into thin strips
⅓ loaf of white bread (made into breadcrumbs)
Seasoned flour
1 teaspoon paprika
2 eggs, beaten
1 tablespoon sunflower oil

METHOD

Heat oil in frying pan. Dust strips of pheasant in flour. Dip into beaten egg and then into breadcrumbs (seasoned and with a pinch of paprika). Fry the nuggets gently until crispy and golden. Serve with fried sliced potatoes and accompany with home-made tomato sauce.

Home-made tomato sauce:
2 tablespoons olive oil
1 finely chopped onion
1 x 15 ozs (450g) tin of tomatoes
Sugar to taste
Teaspoon Lea & Perrins
Seasoning
A pinch of fresh basil/finely chopped parsley

METHOD

Fry finely chopped onion in oil. Add tomatoes and basil. Simmer for 10 minutes. Liquidise. Season. Add sugar and Lea & Perrins to taste. Serve warm or cold.

serves 4

PORK CHOPS WITH GORGONZOLA

Dead easy and tasty.

INGREDIENTS

4 large boneless pork loin chops
1 tablespoon olive oil
1 tablespoon green pesto
3 small tomatoes, thinly sliced
4 ozs (100g) Gorgonzola, cut into 4 thick slices
Seasoning

METHOD

Brush chops with olive oil and season. Lay chops on a baking sheet and grill for 4-5 minutes on one side and again on the other side. Remove from grill. Brush each one with pesto. Place tomato slices on top, then add the cheese. Place chops under the grill again for 2-4 minutes until the cheese is bubbling and melted. Serve with couscous and a herby salad.

Gorgonzola is an Italian cheese variety dating back to the 11th and 12th centuries. It comes from the town of Gorgonzola in Lombardy

serves 4

RACK OF LAMB WITH A PARSLEY & BREADCRUMB TOPPING SERVED WITH A MINT HOLLANDAISE SAUCE

Nothing tastes better than a rack of Spring lamb.

INGREDIENTS

4 x 4-bone racks of lamb
1 oz (25g) fine white breadcrumbs
1 oz (25g) chopped parsley
A pinch of fresh thyme leaves
Seasoning
½ oz (15g) butter
1 beaten egg
2 fl ozs (50ml) Dijon mustard
Pinch garlic

Mint Hollandaise:
4 egg yolks
1 tablespoon water
2 tablespoons lemon juice
6 ozs (150g) melted butter
Seasoning
1 tablespoon finely chopped mint

METHOD

Place breadcrumbs, parsley, thyme, pinch garlic and seasoning in food processor and blend. Add butter to make a paste. Mix egg and mustard together. Coat racks of lamb with egg mix and press parsley mixture onto it. Place in roasting tin and roast at 350°F/180°C/Gas 4 for 20-25 minutes, until lamb is done to your taste. Meanwhile, make sauce. Whisk egg yolks, water and lemon juice in bowl over hot water. Pour in melted butter and whisk till thick. Season and add chopped mint. Serve with duchesse potatoes and courgettes with dill.

PS. If it curdles, add an ice cube and whisk like mad!

RACK OF LAMB WITH THYME & MEAUX MUSTARD EN CROÛTE

A family favourite.

INGREDIENTS

2 whole trimmed racks of lamb
2 tablespoons Meaux mustard
8 sprigs of fresh thyme
Seasoning
2 lbs (900g) puff pastry
1 tablespoon oil

METHOD

Season racks and sear thoroughly in hot oil. Coat racks with Meaux mustard and place thyme leaves on top. Roll out puff pastry to approximately ⅛" (3mm). Encase rack in pastry, sealing openings and brushing all over with egg wash. Place in hot oven 400°F/200°C/Gas 6, for about 30 minutes. Serve with cranberry sauce.

THE LAIRD OF BALLINDALLOCH AND HER FAMILY ~ An oil painting in the Dining Room by Paco Carvajal

serves 4

ROAST SALMON WITH GOAT'S CHEESE AND HERBS ACCOMPANIED BY A CREAM & PRAWN SAUCE

A very special combination.

INGREDIENTS

4 fillets of salmon
Olive oil
Seasoning
4 thin slices of goat's cheese
Chopped herbs

Cream & Prawn Sauce:
½ pt (300ml) double cream
Finely chopped mixed herbs
4 ozs (100g) large prawns

METHOD

Place salmon on a lightly oiled baking sheet and season well. Cook at 425°F/220°C/Gas 7 for 5 minutes. Remove. Place a slice of goat's cheese on top of each fillet then return to oven for a further 2-3 minutes. Meanwhile, make sauce. Heat cream to simmering point, add prawns and sprinkle in herbs. Serve salmon accompanied by the sauce, sprinkled with more chopped herbs.

SMOKED FISH SOUFFLÉ

Perfect for kitchen suppers.

INGREDIENTS

1 lb (450g) smoked haddock
12 ozs (350g) peeled potatoes, cooked and kept warm
3 eggs, separated
2 ozs (50g) butter
3 tablespoons fresh chives
Parsley for garnish
1 tablespoon lemon juice
2 tablespoons white wine
Seasoning

METHOD

Place haddock in pan with cold water and wine to cover. Bring to simmering point over gentle heat and poach fish for 5-7 minutes till flaky. Cool slightly, drain well and remove skin and bones. Mash potatoes well with butter, chives, 3 egg yolks and seasoning. Stir in flaked fish and lemon juice. Whisk egg whites till stiff and fold in gently. Spoon into buttered ovenproof dish. Bake at 350°F/180°C/Gas 4 for 35 minutes till risen and golden. Sprinkle with chopped parsley.

Our Head Ghillie on the Ballindalloch Beat of the River Spey

Ospreys breed in this part of Scotland. They make spectacular dives into lochs and rivers catching salmon and trout.

Detail from a painting by Colin Hunter, 1841-1904

God grant that I may fish until my dying day,
And when I've taken my last cast I then humbly pray,
When in the Lord's safe landing net I am peacefully asleep,
That in his mercy I am judged as good enough to keep.

ROASTED SALMON WITH A CRUNCHY PARMESAN TOPPING

Always a winner.

INGREDIENTS

4 fillets of salmon or plaice (skinned and boned)
2 ozs (50g) freshly grated Parmesan cheese
3 ozs (75g) stale white bread cut into cubes
3 ozs (75g) melted butter + extra for greasing
1 bunch parsley
1 lemon, quartered
Seasoning

Home-made tomato sauce:
2 tablespoons olive oil
1 finely chopped onion
1 x 15 ozs (450g) tin of tomatoes
Sugar to taste
Teaspoon Lea & Perrins
Seasoning
A pinch of fresh basil/finely chopped parsley

METHOD

Line baking tray with foil and brush generously with melted butter. Wipe fish dry with kitchen paper and lay on foil and season. Whizz cubes of bread and parsley leaves in processor till like fine breadcrumbs. Add Parmesan, melted butter and seasoning. Whizz. Spread mixture onto fish, drizzle a little melted butter over. Place in oven at 400ºF/200ºC/Gas 6 for about 8-10 minutes, till golden brown. Serve with a warm tomato sauce.

METHOD

Fry finely chopped onion in oil. Add tomatoes and basil. Simmer for 10 minutes. Liquidise. Season. Add sugar and Lea & Perrins to taste. Serve warm or cold.

serves 6-8

SPICY MINCE WITH A SOUFFLÉ TOP

A lunch dish with a difference.

INGREDIENTS

2 tablespoons oil
2 onions, finely chopped
1 teaspoon chilli powder
2 teaspoons ground coriander
1 teaspoon ground cumin
½ piece fresh root ginger, peeled and grated
1½ lbs (675g) minced Aberdeen Angus beef
2 large tomatoes, chopped
4 eggs, separated
2 teaspoons cornflour
Seasoning
Chopped parsley for garnish

METHOD

Sauté onions in oil in saucepan till soft. Add ginger and spices and fry for 2 minutes. Add mince and stir over high heat till brown. Season. Add ¼ pt (150ml) water and tomatoes and simmer for about 15 minutes till liquid is reduced. (If mince is lumpy, whizz with old-fashioned hand whisk). Place in ovenproof dish. Set aside. Mix egg yolks with cornflour and seasoning. Whisk egg whites till stiff. Fold into egg yolks. Spoon egg mixture over mince and bake at 375°F/190°C/Gas 5 for about 20 minutes until golden and risen. Serve with a mixed salad.

serves 4

STEVE'S CHICKEN

A favourite with the family.

INGREDIENTS

4 chicken breasts
6 ozs (150g) goat's cheese
6-8 slices wholemeal bread (made into breadcrumbs)
2 eggs, beaten
2-3 ozs (50-75g) flour, seasoned
4 tablespoons cooking oil

Mushroom sauce:
1 oz (25g) butter
1 oz (25g) flour
½ pt (300ml) milk
1 lb (450g) sliced mushrooms, fried in butter
Seasoning

METHOD

Slice chicken breast lengthways, not quite all the way through, to make pocket and stuff chicken breasts with goat's cheese. Place seasoned flour, beaten eggs and breadcrumbs in 3 separate bowls. Dip each breast first in flour, then in egg. Let most of the egg drip off then roll chicken in breadcrumbs. Heat oil in non-stick frying pan. Fry chicken breasts till golden on both sides. Take out of pan and place on non-stick tray. Bake at 350°F/180°C/Gas 4 for about 15-20 minutes. Meanwhile, make mushroom sauce. Place butter, flour and milk in pan and whisk like mad over gentle heat till thick and creamy. Season. Add sliced, fried mushrooms. Serve chicken with a blob of mushroom sauce and accompany with new potatoes and a herby salad.

ASPARAGUS & GOAT'S CHEESE TART

Superb as a lunch dish or starter.

INGREDIENTS

Pastry:
4oz (100g) butter
6oz (150g) plain flour
1 teaspoon Parmesan cheese, freshly grated
Seasoning

Filling:
10oz (275g) asparagus, trimmed
2 eggs
200ml carton of crème fraîche
4oz (100g) goat's cheese, cut into chunks

METHOD

Whizz pastry ingredients in processor until they look like fine breadcrumbs. Mould into greased 7" (17.5cm) flan dish. Cool in fridge. Place on hot tray and bake at 350°F/180°C/Gas 4 for 20-25 minutes. Cool. Meanwhile, cut asparagus tips off and place stalks in salted boiling water. Cook for 5-6 minutes until soft. Remove with slotted spoon and set aside. Place asparagus tips in the boiling water and blanche for 2 minutes. Place chopped asparagus stalks, eggs and crème fraîche in liquidiser and whizz until smooth. Season and pour into flan case. Sprinkle the asparagus tips and chunks of goat's cheese over mixture and bake at 400°F/200°C/Gas 6 for about 40 minutes until slightly brown. Serve warm with a herby salad.

serves 6

SPINACH & GRUYÈRE TART

Perfect for a quick supper.

INGREDIENTS

Pastry:
4 ozs (100g) butter
6 ozs (150g) plain flour
1 teaspoon Parmesan cheese, freshly grated
Seasoning

Filling:
2 lbs (900g) spinach, washed
½ pt (300ml) whipping cream
3 eggs
Seasoning
Nutmeg, freshly grated
8 ozs (225g) Gruyère, freshly grated
5 ozs (125g) cherry tomatoes, halved
Groundnut oil

METHOD

Whizz pastry ingredients in processor until the mixture is like fine breadcrumbs. Mould into greased 7" (17.5cm) flan dish. Cool in fridge. Place on hot tray and bake at 350°F/180°C/Gas 4 for 20-25 minutes. Cool. Place spinach in a large saucepan with just the water you have washed it in. Cover with lid and cook over medium heat for about 10 minutes until it wilts. Drain spinach by placing in colander and squeezing with potato masher until there is no water left. Leave to cool and drain further. Squeeze again, place on chopping board and chop into small pieces. In a bowl whisk together the cream, eggs and seasoning. Add a little grated nutmeg and stir in the spinach well. Add half the Gruyère. Pour into pastry case and smooth over. Toss in a bowl the halved cherry tomatoes with the groundnut oil. Scatter over the surface of the flan and sprinkle with the rest of the Gruyère cheese. Bake at 375°F/190°C/Gas 5 for about 35 minutes, until set.

serves 4

WILD DUCK WITH SPICY MANGO SAUCE

In Guy's words – "an awesome combo"!

INGREDIENTS

2 wild ducks
1 orange
Knob butter

Sauce:
1 onion (finely sliced)
2 tablespoons oil
2 cloves garlic, peeled and chopped
2 fresh mangoes (skinned and stoned) or 1 tin
1 teaspoon freshly grated root ginger
1 dessertspoon redcurrant jelly
Large dash soy sauce
Seasoning
Juice and zest of 1 orange

METHOD

Place halved orange in both ducks and rub all over with butter. Place duck in tin with tablespoon of water. Roast at 400°F/200°C/Gas 6 for 15 minutes – they should still be pink inside. Meanwhile, make sauce. Heat oil and fry onion and garlic till translucent. Add grated ginger, juice and zest of one orange, sliced mango and soy sauce. Stir, season and keep warm. Slice breasts of duck and plate individually in a fan shape on a bed of creamed celeriac surrounded by mango sauce.

serves 4

STUFFED CROISSANTS

I could eat these every day.

INGREDIENTS

4 croissants
4 slices good home-baked ham, diced
¼ pt (150ml) soured cream
4 oz (100g) Emmental cheese, grated
1 teaspoon English mustard

METHOD

Cut a lid out of the top of the croissants and make a well. Mix soured cream and mustard together. Add grated cheese and chopped ham. Stuff croissants with mixture and bake at 350°F/180°C/Gas 4, for about 15 minutes. Serve with a herb salad.

Swiss Emmental cheese –
full of holes and so less fattening?!

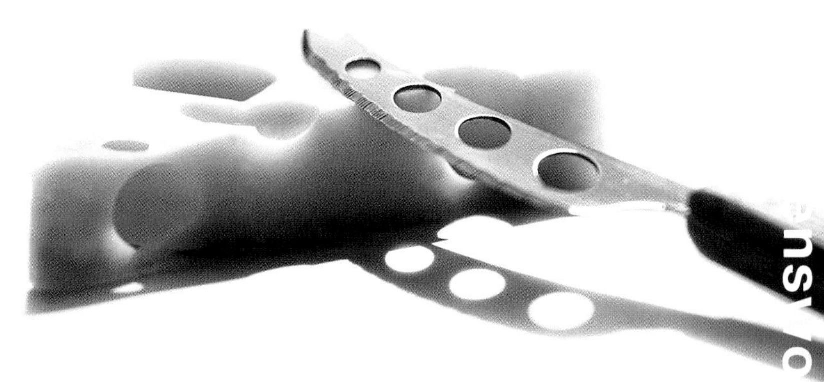

serves 4

FILLET OF BEEF WITH THYME, PORT & HONEY

Perfect use for 1975 port!

INGREDIENTS

4 x 6 oz (175g) Aberdeen Angus fillet steaks
1 tablespoon olive oil
1 bunch fresh thyme, finely chopped
4 fl ozs (120ml) red wine
2 ozs (50g) shiitake mushrooms
2 teaspoons runny honey
4 fl ozs (120ml) port

METHOD

Heat oil in large, heavy frying pan. Sprinkle in thyme and add steaks. Cook for about 2-3 minutes on each side (or to taste). Take out steaks with slotted spoon and keep warm. Add wine and mushrooms and reduce liquid by half. Add honey and port and reduce again by half. Serve steaks with a little sauce spooned over them and accompanied by potato dauphinois and fresh asparagus.

serves 4

ROAST FILLET OF PORK STUFFED WITH STILTON CHEESE

Lovely way of using up ageing Stilton.

INGREDIENTS

2 pork fillets, 1 lb (450g) total
2 ozs (50g) Stilton cheese
1 tablespoon plain flour
1 oz (25g) butter
1 tablespoon olive oil
4 tablespoons white wine
1 small bunch green grapes
Sage leaves
Seasoning

METHOD

Make cut along each fillet and stuff with sliced Stilton and sage leaves. Tie with string and dust with seasoned flour. Heat butter and oil in large frying pan and seal pork on all sides till brown. Add wine and bring to boil. Place in roasting pan and bake at 400ºF/200ºC/Gas 6 for about 30 minutes. To serve, untie string, slice pork into 1" (2.5cm) pieces and place on plate. Keep warm. Heat juices left in pan, season, add halved grapes and warm. Drizzle over pork. Serve with brown organic rice and mangetout.

sage in flower

GINGER SALMON

These ingredients go really well together.

INGREDIENTS

4 fillets of salmon
Juice of 2 limes
3 tablespoons sunflower oil
1 onion, peeled and chopped
2 teaspoons grated root ginger
6 ozs (150g) mangetout
Soy sauce
Seasoning

For Ginger Sauce:
2 tablespoons runny honey
1 teaspoon grated root ginger
Juice of one lime

METHOD

Place salmon fillets in dish and sprinkle with lime juice. Leave, covered, for 15 minutes. Heat heavy frying pan and add 2 tablespoons oil. Place salmon fillets in pan and season. Cook for few minutes on each side till just pink in middle. Keep warm. Stir-fry mangetout, onion and ginger together. Season with a dash of soy sauce. Set aside and keep warm. For sauce, gently heat honey in pan with grated root ginger, lime juice and seasoning. To serve, place salmon on bed of mangetout and drizzle with sauce.

Watercolour of the Castle in the 18th century

COLLOPS OF PORK FILLET WITH CREAM, CALVADOS & APPLE SAUCE

Very rich, but the apple balances it well.

INGREDIENTS

4 pork fillets, trimmed
2 eating apples
Juice and zest of 1 lemon
1 tablespoon oil
2 ozs (50g) butter
3 fl ozs (75ml) Calvados
½ pt (300ml) double cream
Seasoning

METHOD

Peel, core and slice apples and sprinkle with lemon juice and zest. Cut fillet into 1" (2.5cm) thick medallions, and flatten with rolling pin. Heat oil and butter in large pan, add collops and cook on both sides for about 4-5 minutes, till brown but still slightly pink inside. Pour over Calvados and ignite with a match. Take off heat and, after a few seconds, pour cream over top. Drain apple slices and add to pork. Cook for about 3 minutes. Serve with couscous and a green vegetable.

Watercolour of the Castle in 2000 by Liz Graydon

grey or common partridge

Archibald Thorburn is considered by many to be the greatest ever bird artist. This exquisite watercolour portrays Britain's indigenous partridge. Far from 'common', it has been in decline since the introduction of pesticides and changes in farming methods in the 1950s. Happily, this traditional gamebird is now in the process of recovering some of its original population.

FRICASSÉE OF PARTRIDGE BREAST SERVED ON FRIED BREAD WITH A PARSLEY CREAM SAUCE, SPRINKLED WITH BACON

The dish for a special occasion.

INGREDIENTS

8 partridge breasts
8 slices of bacon, chopped
1oz (25g) butter
½ pt (300ml) double cream
4 slices of fried bread
Bunch of parsley
Seasoning
1 small onion, finely chopped

METHOD

Fry off bacon until crispy and keep hot. Fry off croutons and keep hot. Melt butter, fry partridge breast and onion together on medium heat for 3 minutes each side. Add double cream and chopped parsley, then simmer until cream thickens. Season. Serve individually. Place crouton on plate. Place partridge on crouton, spoon over sauce. Sprinkle with bacon and chopped parsley.

serves 6

BALLINDALLOCH BIRDIE GAME PIE

Wonderful for smart picnics or buffets.

INGREDIENTS

Hot Water Crust Pastry:
10 ozs (300g) plain white flour
¼ teaspoon salt
¼ pt (150ml) water
2 ozs (50g) white vegetable fat

Filling:
8 ozs (225g) duck/partridge breasts (skinned and boned)
8 ozs (225g) loin of roe deer/venison
1 pt (600ml) chicken stock
8 ozs (225g) pork sausagemeat
1 onion, finely chopped
4 tablespoons sherry
8 ozs (225g) pheasant breasts (skinned and boned)
3 ozs (75g) ready-to-eat dried apricots
3 ozs (75g) ready-to-eat prunes
3 ozs (75g) tinned chestnuts
Seasoning and garlic to taste
8 fresh sage leaves
1 teaspoon (5ml) powdered gelatine

METHOD

Cut the duck/partridge breasts and loin of venison into small pieces and place in pan with stock. Bring to simmering point over medium heat and cook for about 20 minutes till tender. Remove with slotted spoon and set aside. Boil stock, reducing to ¼ pt (150ml), and reserve. Line a collapsible terrine mould with non-stick baking parchment. In bowl mix together cooked meats, sausagemeat, finely chopped onion, garlic to taste, sherry and seasoning. Cover and refrigerate.

Make pastry by first sifting flour and salt in bowl. Make well in middle. Slowly heat fat and water together till fat melts. Bring to boil and pour into well. Lightly knead against side of bowl into smooth ball. Wrap dough into tea towel and rest for ten minutes. Roll out ¾ of pastry to cover 12 x 16 inches (30 x 40 cm), using rolling pin to lift into tin. Mould pastry into tin and bake blind at 400ºF/200ºC/Gas 6 for about 15-20 minutes till golden and set.

Remove paper and beans.
Cool. Spoon half of game mixture into pastry case and scatter with half the chopped apricots/prunes/ chestnuts. Lay pheasant breasts on top and dot with sage leaves. Scatter over rest of fruit and nut mixture. Roll out remaining pastry to cover lid. Place over top and press edges together to seal. Trim and flute edges. Make 3 large holes with wooden spoon in pie lid. Decorate top with pastry trimmings. Glaze with beaten egg. Place on baking tray and bake at 400ºF/200ºC/Gas 6 for 20 minutes. Lower setting to 350ºF/180ºC/Gas 4 for further 1 hour and cover top with foil. Take out and fold flaps of tin down. Cook for further 20 minutes to brown sides. Cool. Soak gelatine in 4 teaspoons water. Heat reserved stock and gradually add to gelatine. Stir till dissolved. Cool till almost setting. Remove pie from tin. Place on lipped plate and gradually pour stock into holes. Refrigerate overnight.

puds

- FAVOURITE DESSERTS

puds - FAVOURITE DESSERTS

In the corridor leading to the Nursery are two examples of the Lady Laird's early work!

serves 6

BERRY SHORTBREAD

A big cheat when time is not on your side.

INGREDIENTS

6 thin shortbread biscuits
6 ozs (150g) mascarpone
6 ozs (150g) fresh berries – strawberries, raspberries or blueberries
2 teaspoons runny honey and
1 teaspoon thick honey
Icing sugar for decoration

Raspberry Coulis:
8 ozs (225g) raspberries, liquidised and sieved, with sugar to taste

METHOD

Mix mascarpone gently with runny honey. Spread onto shortbread biscuits. Arrange berries on top. Place shortbreads on individual plates, anchored with a little thick honey. Dust with icing sugar and serve with a raspberry coulis.

serves 6-8

APPLE & BANANA CRUMBLE

A lovely crunch on top and deliciously squidgy underneath - a superb recipe given to me by Joan Irvine

INGREDIENTS

4 ozs (100g) butter
8 ozs (225g) soft brown sugar
5 ozs (125g) plain flour
1 teaspoon ground cinnamon
3 ozs (75g) walnut pieces
1½ lbs (675g) cooking apples
3-4 medium size bananas
Juice of 1 lemon
3 ozs (75g) caster sugar

METHOD

Peel and slice fruit into a bowl, add caster sugar and lemon juice and mix up well. Grease a 2pt ovenproof pie dish and then tip in the fruit mixture. Gently melt the butter. Put the dry ingredients into a bowl and stir in the melted butter until well mixed. Spoon onto fruit. Bake at 350°F/180°C/Gas 4 for about 1 hour. If the top looks as though it is getting too brown, lay a piece of foil loosely over the top.

CARAMELISED BANANA TARTLETS

Looks stunning and is delectable.

INGREDIENTS

2 ozs (50g) butter, melted
8 sheets of filo pastry
4 tablespoons icing sugar, plus extra for dusting
½ pt (300ml) double cream

Caramelised Bananas:
4 ozs (100g) caster sugar
3 large bananas, peeled and cut into 1" (2.5cm) chunks

METHOD

Lightly brush a baking sheet with a little melted butter. Place one sheet of filo pastry on a pastry board and brush with melted butter, then another sheet on top and brush with butter and 1 tablespoon of icing sugar. Then place a third sheet of filo pastry on top, and again brush with melted butter, then a fourth with melted butter and a tablespoon of icing sugar. Repeat this to create another pile with the rest of the filo pastry. Cut out 3 x 3" (7.5cm) circles from each filo stack. Place on prepared baking sheet and bake at 350°F/180°C/Gas 4 for 5-7 minutes. Remove from oven and cool. Whip cream and set aside. Heat caster sugar in heavy-based frying pan over high heat until it dissolves. Add banana chunks and cook for 1 minute. To assemble, place a circle of filo on each plate. Top with double cream, then a spoonful of bananas then another filo, cream and bananas. Top with third filo and dust with icing sugar. Drizzle a little caramel on the plate and a few segments of fresh orange.

serves 6

BLACKBERRY/RASPBERRY & APPLE SOUFFLÉ

Dreamy – light as a feather.

INGREDIENTS

6 ozs (150g) caster sugar
12 ozs (350g) blackberries + 24 for bottom of soufflé
1 large cooking apple, peeled and finely diced
Zest and juice of 1 orange
3 egg whites
½ pt (300ml) double cream
Icing sugar for dusting

METHOD

Cook blackberries, diced apple, zest and juice of orange in pan for 10 minutes, until apple is pulp. Press through sieve into bowl. Stir in 2 ozs (50g) of caster sugar. Cool. Place spoonful of fruit purée and 4 blackberries into bottom of 6 ramekins (buttered and dusted with sugar). Set aside. Whisk egg whites till very stiff. Gradually whisk in remaining sugar till glossy. Fold in remaining fruit purée and pour into ramekins. Level the tops and run knife around edges of each dish. Place on hot baking tray (to make rise) and bake at 400°F/200°C/Gas 6 for about 10-15 minutes till risen and lightly brown. Dust tops with icing sugar and serve immediately with jug of double cream.

serves 4-6

CHOCOLATE ICE-CREAM

Ice-creams are not only the best to eat, but the best for the working lady.

INGREDIENTS

½ pt (300ml) single cream
3 egg yolks
3 tablespoons caster sugar
2 teaspoons cornflour
½ pt (300ml) double cream, whipped
6 ozs (150g) plain chocolate, melted in bowl over pan of hot water
2 tablespoons cocoa
1 chocolate flake
Walkers of Aberlour 'Ginger Thins'

METHOD

Place single cream in pan and bring to boil. Turn off heat. Whisk together eggs, sugar and cornflour till pale and creamy. Whisk single cream into egg mixture. Add melted chocolate and cocoa powder. Return to pan and bring to simmering point over moderate heat. Cook gently till custard coats back of wooden spoon – DO NOT BOIL, or you will have scrambled eggs! Cool completely. Then whisk well and fold in whipped double cream and crumbled flake. Place in container in freezer and whisk twice in 2 hours, or make in ice-cream maker. To serve, take out half hour before required. Accompany ice-cream with 'Ginger Thins' made by Walkers of Aberlour.

serves 6

CHOCOLATE & ORANGE MOUSSE

These two flavours are perfect together.

INGREDIENTS

7 ozs (175g) orange flavoured dark chocolate, broken into pieces
½ oz (15g) unsalted butter
1 tablespoon Cointreau
4 large eggs (separated)
Zest of 1 orange
¼ pt (150ml) whipped double cream

METHOD

Place chocolate pieces and butter in bowl with 4 tablespoons cold water and place over a pan of hot water. Leave till chocolate has melted, stirring occasionally. Remove from heat and cool slightly. Stir in Cointreau and set aside. Whisk egg whites till stiff. Stir egg yolks into chocolate mixture. Add a spoonful of egg white, then fold in the remaining egg whites a little at a time with a metal spoon. Spoon into glass dishes and chill for several hours. Decorate with orange zest and a blob of whipped cream.

serves 6

COLD LEMON SOUFFLÉ WITH ALMONDS

An old favourite but a wonderful palate-cleaner to end a meal.

INGREDIENTS

6 medium eggs, separated
2 sachets of gelatine
Zest and juice of 3 large lemons
4 ozs (100g) caster sugar
¾ pt (450ml) double cream

Almond Topping:
3 ozs (75g) flaked almonds
3 ozs (75g) icing sugar

METHOD

Butter and dust 8 ramekins with sugar. Wrap a piece of buttered greaseproof paper around each dish, standing about one inch above edge of ramekin. Secure firmly with tape. Place zest of lemons and egg yolks in bowl. Add 3 ozs (75g) of caster sugar and whisk till light in colour and creamy. Set aside. Place lemon juice in small bowl and sprinkle with gelatine. Place bowl over pan of simmering water until gelatine is melted and clear. Cool slightly. Stir gelatine and lemon juice into egg yolk mixture. Set aside. In separate bowl, lightly whip cream. Fold into egg mixture and set aside. Whisk egg whites till stiff. Gradually whisk in remaining caster sugar till stiff and glossy. Quickly and gently fold the whites into egg yolk mixture. Pour into prepared ramekins and chill for 4-5 hours. (To serve iced, place in freezer and take out about ten minutes before serving). Meanwhile, make almond topping. Brush baking sheet lightly with oil. Scatter almonds across baking sheet and sift icing sugar over. Grill until nuts turn golden-brown and sugar has caramelised. Cool, then break almond mixture into small pieces. When soufflé has set, peel off paper and sprinkle with almonds.

Queen Charlotte by Allan Ramsay, 1713 - 1784. This painting and the accompanying one of King George III were presented to General James Grant in recognition of his military services in the American Wars of Independence. They now hang in the Dining Room at the Castle.

CHOCOLATE QUEEN OF PUDDINGS

A real old-fashioned favourite, modernised for chocoholics. It was made popular by Queen Charlotte. Her Majesty considered it a nutritious and economical dish to serve patients at her hospital. To honour the Queen the meringue was piped around the sides to give an impression of a crown.

→

serves 4-6

INGREDIENTS

2 ozs (50g) dark chocolate
¾ pt (450ml) chocolate-flavoured milk
4 ozs (100g) white breadcrumbs
5 ozs (125g) caster sugar
3 eggs, separated

METHOD

Break chocolate into small pieces. Place in pan with chocolate milk. Heat gently, stirring, till chocolate is melted. Bring almost to the boil then remove from heat. Place breadcrumbs in large mixing bowl with 1 oz (25g) sugar. Pour over the chocolate milk and mix well. Beat in egg yolks. Spoon into 2 pt (1.1 litre) oval pie dish and bake at 350°F/180°C/Gas 4 for 25-30 minutes till set and firm to touch. Whisk egg whites in large bowl till in soft peaks. Whisk in remaining sugar. Spread over chocolate mixture. Return pudding to oven for about 15 minutes.

CHOCOLATE ORANGE SOUFFLÉS SERVED WITH WHITE CHOCOLATE SAUCE

Scrumptious - both easy and dramatic.

INGREDIENTS

3 tablespoons caster sugar
6 ozs (175g) good plain chocolate, chopped
5 ozs (125g) unsalted butter, cut into pieces
4 large eggs, separated
2 tablespoons orange liqueur
¼ teaspoon cream of tartar

White Chocolate Sauce:
3 ozs (75g) white chocolate, chopped
½ pt (300ml) whipping cream
2 tablespoons orange liqueur
Zest of 1 orange

METHOD

Melt chocolate and butter in bowl over pan of simmering water. Remove from heat, cool slightly. Beat in egg yolks and orange liqueur. Set aside. Whisk egg whites till frothy. Add cream of tartar. Whisk again till in soft peaks. Gradually add caster sugar a tablespoon at a time, whisking till whites are stiff. Stir a third of the whisked whites into cooled chocolate mixture then pour the mixture over the remaining whites. Fold the sauce gently into whites with metal spoon. Spoon mixture into buttered ramekins. Place ramekins on hot baking tray, knife around the edge of ramekins and bake at 425°F/220°C/Gas 7 for about 10-12 minutes till risen and set. Meanwhile, make white chocolate sauce. Place chopped white chocolate in pan with liqueur and zest of 1 orange. Heat till melted and then add whipping cream and re-heat. Take soufflés out of oven and dust with icing sugar. Make hole in middle of each soufflé, pour in white chocolate sauce and serve as quickly as possible.

serves 6

FRESH RASPBERRY TARTLETS

Raspberries conjure up the feeling of hot summer days.

INGREDIENTS

4 ozs (100g) butter
6 ozs (150g) plain flour
1 teaspoon icing sugar

For filling:
3 tablespoons home-made raspberry jam
½ pt (300ml) double cream
1 lb (450g) fresh raspberries
¼ pt (150ml) redcurrant jelly
3 ozs (75g) melted white chocolate

METHOD

Whizz pastry ingredients in processor until like fine breadcrumbs. Mould into 6 greased individual tartlet moulds and cool in fridge. Place on hot tray and bake at 350°F/180°C/Gas 4 for 20-25 minutes. Cool. Meanwhile, make filling by pressing raspberry jam through a sieve into a bowl, to remove the seeds. Add cream and whisk until thick. Melt white chocolate in a bowl over a pan of hot water. Brush the inside of the tartlet cases with chocolate to stop them going soggy. Cool to harden. Spoon the cream mixture into the tartlets and cover with fresh raspberries. Warm redcurrant jelly in a pan until melted and brush over raspberries to glaze. Refrigerate for 10 minutes and serve.

serves 6

HIGHLAND BRULÉE

Temptingly easy to prepare.

INGREDIENTS

1 large Toblerone bar
1 pint (600ml) double cream
8 ozs (225g) raspberries
Granulated sugar for brulée tops

METHOD

Melt Toblerone in bowl over pan of gently simmering water. Allow to cool slightly. Whip double cream and add melted chocolate. Place fresh raspberries at bottom of ramekins and pour chocolate mix over. Place in deep freeze for one hour. Take out and cover with granulated sugar, then brulée the tops with a blowtorch. Serve.

The Highlander atop the turret guards the Castle

ICED WHITE CHOCOLATE TERRINE WITH RASPBERRY COULIS

Another scrumptious chocolate combination!

INGREDIENTS

2 tablespoons granulated sugar
5 tablespoons water
10 ozs (275g) white chocolate
3 eggs, separated
½ pt (300ml) double cream
1 punnet of strawberries to decorate

Raspberry Coulis:
8 ozs (225g) raspberries (or strawberries)
1-2 tablespoons icing sugar

METHOD

Place sugar and water in heavy-based pan and heat gently, stirring till sugar has dissolved. Bring to boil and boil for 1-2 minutes till syrupy. Remove from heat. Break white chocolate into small pieces and stir into syrup till melted. Cool slightly. Beat egg yolks into chocolate mixture. Cool. Whip cream and fold into mixture. Whisk egg whites till standing in 'soft peaks'. Fold in chocolate mixture. Pour into 1 lb (450g) bread tin lined with cling film and freeze overnight. To serve, remove from freezer about 10-15 minutes before required. Meanwhile make raspberry coulis. Whizz fruit and icing sugar in blender. Sieve. Turn terrine out of tin and slice. Serve two slices on plate surrounded with raspberry coulis and a strawberry.

serves 6-8

LEMON TART SERVED WITH AN ORANGE AND KIWI SALAD

Loved by all – fruit flavours galore.

INGREDIENTS

6 ozs (150g) plain flour, sifted
2 ozs (50g) hazelnuts, toasted and finely ground
6 ozs (150g) caster sugar
4 ozs (100g) butter, softened
4 large eggs
Zest and juice of 2 large lemons
¼ pt (150ml) double cream
Crème fraîche for decoration

For orange and kiwi salad:
8 oranges, peeled and segmented
6 kiwi fruit, peeled and sliced
Sugar to taste

METHOD

Mix together flour, nuts and two tablespoons sugar. Gently work in butter and, if necessary, add 1 tablespoon cold water to make soft dough. Chill for ten minutes in fridge. Roll out dough onto floured board and press into 8" (20cm) loose-based flan tin. Chill for another 20 minutes. Line pastry case with greaseproof paper and fill with baking beans. Bake at 400°F/200°C/Gas 6 for 15 minutes till base is crisp. Beat eggs, lemon zest, lemon juice, remaining sugar and cream till well mixed. Pour into pastry case and bake at 350°F/180°C/Gas 4 for about 30 minutes till set. Serve in individual slices, accompanied by a few slices of fresh orange and kiwis on the side and a blob of crème fraîche.

serves 6

NORWEGIAN CREAM

An ancient recipe from one of the old Ballindalloch Castle cookbooks.

INGREDIENTS

1 pt (600ml) full-cream milk
½ pt (300ml) single cream
Vanilla essence
2 whole eggs
5 egg yolks
1 tablespoon caster sugar
¼ pt (150ml) double cream
2-3 tablespoons apricot jam
Grated Bournville chocolate for decoration

METHOD

Spoon apricot jam into bottom of soufflé dish. Heat milk and single cream in pan to boiling point. Beat eggs and egg yolks with caster sugar and add a few drops of vanilla essence. Mix a little of the hot milk/cream into egg mixture and then add the rest. Pour mixture on top of apricot jam. Place soufflé dish in bain-marie (a baking tin half filled with hot water) and bake at 325°F/170°C/Gas 3 for about 35 minutes till set. Cool. When chilled, cover with whipped double cream and sprinkle with chocolate.

'General James Grant in 1798 - obviously a great fan of puds!'

ORANGE/GRAPEFRUIT TART

A favourite with young and old.

INGREDIENTS

Pastry:
4 ozs (100g) butter
6 ozs (150g) plain flour
1 teaspoon icing sugar

Filling:
7 fl ozs (180ml) freshly-squeezed orange/grapefruit juice
8 ozs (225g) golden caster sugar
5 large eggs, beaten
7 fl ozs (180ml) double cream
4 oranges and 2 grapefruit, peeled and segmented, for decoration

METHOD

Whizz pastry ingredients till like fine breadcrumbs. Mould into 7" (17.5cm) flan dish. Cool in fridge. Place on hot tray and bake at 350°F/180°C/Gas 4 for 20-25 minutes. Cool.

Filling:
Strain fruit juice into bowl and beat in sugar till dissolved. Push eggs through sieve into bowl of orange juice. Mix and fold in cream.
Pour mixture into flan case. Bake at 325°F/170°C/Gas 3 for about 40-45 minutes. Cool and serve with a cream and Drambuie sauce, decorated with segments of orange and grapefruit.

Cream & Drambuie sauce:
Blend together ½ pt (300ml) double cream, 1 tablespoon Drambuie and sugar to taste.

serves 4

ORANGE CRÈME CARAMEL

Mimi loves this!

INGREDIENTS

5 egg yolks plus 1 egg
6 ozs (150g) caster sugar
1 orange and 1 grapefruit, in segments
¾ pt (450ml) double cream
½ pt (300ml) full-fat milk
4 teaspoons water
Zest of 1 orange

METHOD

Mix together egg yolks, egg and half the sugar in bowl. Bring cream, milk and orange zest to boil in large pan. Remove from heat and cool for 10 minutes. Pour cream mixture over eggs and stir lightly with wooden spoon. Set aside. Melt rest of sugar in small pan over low heat till it begins to darken in colour. Remove from heat and stir in water very carefully to prevent sugar spitting and burning your skin. Pour into bottom of 4 ramekins. Cool. Fill with orange custard. Place in bain-marie (a roasting tin half filled with hot water) and bake at 300°F/150°C/Gas 2 for about 40 minutes till set. Cool. Chill in fridge for about 8 hours. To serve, slide knife round the edge and invert onto plate. Serve with orange and grapefruit segments.

Mimi and our son Edward on their wedding day

serves 4

PASSION FRUIT DREAMS

Mouthwatering – a deliciously creamy, velvet mixture.

INGREDIENTS

1 pt (600ml) double cream
Few drops vanilla essence
6 passion fruits
3 tablespoons sugar
5 eggs
2 tablespoons good lemon curd
Mint leaves and few raspberries for decoration

METHOD

Bring cream and vanilla essence to boiling point. Set aside. Sieve the flesh of 4 passion fruits and beat together with sugar, eggs and lemon curd. Whisk in the hot cream. Pour into lightly buttered ramekins with circles of greaseproof paper at base. Place in bain-marie (a roasting tin half filled with boiling water) and bake at 350°F/180°C/Gas 4 for about 25-30 minutes till set. Cool and chill in fridge for few hours. Before serving, run knife round rim of ramekins and invert onto individual plates. Peel off greaseproof paper. Drizzle flesh of remaining two passion fruit over the pudding and decorate with mint leaves and a raspberry.

RASPBERRY & DRAMBUIE TART

A summer pudding 'par extraordinaire'.

INGREDIENTS

Pastry:
4 ozs (100g) butter
6 ozs (150g) plain flour
2 ozs (50g) ground almonds
1 teaspoon icing sugar

Filling:
1 x 200ml tub crème fraîche (plus 4 tablespoons for serving)
4 tablespoons Drambuie
9 ozs (250g) fresh raspberries
3 tablespoons sugar
2 large eggs

METHOD

Whizz pastry ingredients in processor until like fine breadcrumbs. Mould into 7" (17.5 cm) flan dish. Cool in fridge. Place on hot tray and bake at 350°F/180°C/Gas 4 for 20-25 minutes. Cool. Beat together the sugar, eggs, the 200ml of crème fraîche and 2 tablespoons of Drambuie. Pour the mixture into the pastry case and arrange raspberries on top. Bake in oven at 375°F/190°C/Gas 5 for about 35 minutes, until just set. Beat the remaining crème fraîche and 2 tablespoons of Drambuie together and serve with the warm tart.

serves 6

SCOTTISH BERRY BRULÉE

Straightforward but sensuous!

INGREDIENTS

1 lb (450g) strawberries
8 ozs (225g) raspberries
4 ozs (100g) blueberries
2 tablespoons caster sugar
Grated zest and juice of 1 orange
7 ozs (175g) Greek yogurt
7 fl ozs (180ml) tub of crème fraîche
3 tablespoons soft brown sugar
Few pinches ground cinnamon

METHOD

Place strawberries, raspberries and blueberries in ovenproof dish. Sprinkle over 1 tablespoon of caster sugar and grated zest and juice of 1 orange. Mix together yogurt, crème fraîche and remaining caster sugar. Spread over fruit and leave in fridge for 2 hours. Sprinkle Demerara sugar and cinnamon over top and place under grill till sugar melts. Serve immediately.

by Sir George Hayter (1792-1871)

Sir George Macpherson-Grant, 1st Baronet of Ballindalloch, who turned down a 'Peerage' and became a baronet so that he could still sit in the House of Commons

STEAMED CHOCOLATE PUDDINGS WITH VANILLA SAUCE

Not just for the nursery – for the front cover as well!

INGREDIENTS

3 ozs (75g) butter
4 ozs (100g) soft light brown sugar
¼ pt (150ml) full-cream milk
3 medium eggs, separated
4 ozs (100g) Bournville plain chocolate, chopped
6 ozs (150g) fresh white breadcrumbs
Grated chocolate for decoration

Vanilla Sauce:
4 medium egg yolks
3 ozs (75g) caster sugar
1 pt (600ml) single cream
½ teaspoon cornflour
½ teaspoon vanilla essence

METHOD

Cream butter and sugar till light and fluffy. Beat in 3 egg yolks, one by one. Melt chocolate in pan of milk over gentle heat. Cool slightly and fold in egg mixture alternately with breadcrumbs. Whisk 3 egg whites till stiff and fold into mixture. Pour into 6-8 buttered dariole moulds till ¾ way up sides. Place in bain-marie (a roasting tin half filled with hot water) and cover with buttered tin foil. Bake at 350°F/180°C/Gas 4 for about 35-40 minutes. Meanwhile, make vanilla sauce. Heat cream gently in pan to just boiling point. Whisk together egg yolks, sugar, cornflour and vanilla essence. Pour on a little hot cream and mix well. Return all to pan. Stir very gently over heat till sauce thickens. Do not boil. Uncover chocolate puddings and invert onto plate. Serve with warm vanilla sauce. Decorate with a little grated chocolate.

serves 6-8

STEVE'S CHOCOLATE CHEESECAKE

So easy and so delicious – a total disaster for the figure-conscious!

INGREDIENTS

12 ozs chocolate digestive biscuits or Hobnobs
3 ozs (75g) butter

Filling:
¾ pt (450ml) double cream
1 large tin condensed milk
4 tablespoons cocoa powder
8 ozs (225g) Bournville chocolate
8 ozs (225g) cream cheese
Grated chocolate and raspberries for decoration

METHOD

Melt butter and mix in crushed biscuits. Line bottom of spring-loaded cake tin with mixture and cool in fridge for ½ hour. Melt chocolate in bowl over pan of simmering water. Meanwhile, whisk all rest of ingredients together. Pour in melted chocolate and whisk till thick. Pour onto biscuit base. Place in fridge for several hours. Turn out of tin and decorate with grated chocolate and a few raspberries.

Steve in his office!

serves 4

TOFFEE CRUNCH ICE-CREAM

Truly addictive – throw the scales away!

INGREDIENTS

1 tin condensed milk
½ pt (300ml) double cream
6 ozs (150g) chocolate Hobnobs, crushed
Extra ¼ pt (150ml) double cream + grated chocolate / flake for decoration

METHOD

Boil condensed milk, unopened and completely covered with water, for about 2 hours. Cool overnight. Whisk cream till thick, then add caramelised condensed milk, one spoonful at a time. Mix well. Place in ramekins, layering the mixture with the crushed chocolate biscuits. Freeze for about 2 hours. Take out ½ hour before serving and decorate with the extra whipped double cream and grated chocolate / flake.

P.S. Don't forget (as I once did) to remove condensed milk from heat when ready, otherwise you will have caramel-coated walls!

A glorious winter morning on the River Avon

serves 6

FUDGE PIE

A recipe using Edward's 'Happy Cow' condensed milk – you will have to book a flight to Burma to buy it!

INGREDIENTS

Pastry:
4 ozs (100g) butter
6 ozs (150g) plain flour
1 teaspoon icing sugar

Filling:
1 x 14 ozs (400g) tin 'Happy Cow' condensed milk (you might have to substitute Nestlé's!)
½ pt (300ml) double cream
6 bananas
Bournville chocolate to decorate

METHOD

Whizz pastry ingredients in processor till like fine breadcrumbs. Mould into 7" (17.5 cm) flan dish. Cool in fridge. Place on hot tray and bake at 350°F/180°C/Gas 4 for 20-25 minutes. Cool. Boil Nestlé milk in tin in covered saucepan of water for 2 hours. Cool. Pour fudge from tin into pastry case. Add layer of sliced bananas, then whipped cream. Decorate with grated chocolate.

serves 6

TWICE BAKED CHOCOLATE SOUFFLÉS

Trying to impress? Looks sensational, can be prepared the day before and cooked at the last moment.

INGREDIENTS

2 ozs (50g) butter
1 oz (25g) plain flour
1 oz (25g) cornflour
2 ozs (50g) sugar
1 oz (25g) cocoa powder
½ pt (300ml) milk
5 eggs, separated
6 squares Bournville chocolate
Crème fraîche for decoration

Chocolate Sauce:
¾ pt (450ml) double cream
2 ozs (50g) butter
8 ozs (225g) Bournville chocolate

METHOD

Put everything except eggs, milk and Bournville chocolate in pan. Cook over a warm heat, stirring all the time to make a roux. Slowly add the milk, whisking all the time to make a thick sauce. Take off heat and leave for 2-3 minutes, then whisk in egg yolks. In clean bowl whisk egg whites till stiff. Whisk one heaped tablespoon of egg white into mixture to loosen, then fold in remaining egg whites. Pour into buttered ramekins and cook in a bain-marie (a roasting tin half filled with hot water) in pre-heated oven at 350°F/180°C/Gas 4 for about 15 minutes. Take out of oven and leave for 15 minutes. Run round edge with knife and turn out onto non-stick tray. Push piece of Bournville chocolate into centre of each soufflé. Cover. Place in fridge for 4-6 hours. Meanwhile, make chocolate sauce by placing all ingredients into pan and heating gently till melted. To serve, place each soufflé onto individual ear-dishes, surround with chocolate sauce. Bake at 400°F/200°C/Gas 6 for 12-15 minutes. Serve immediately with blob of crème fraîche.

TWICE BAKED LEMON SOUFFLÉS WITH A CREAMY LEMON SAUCE

Irresistible.

INGREDIENTS

9 oz (250g) fromage frais
4 large eggs, separated
1 oz (25g) cornflour
4 ozs (100g) caster sugar
Grated rind and juice of 1 large lemon

Lemon Sauce:
½ pt (300ml) double cream
1 tablespoon lemon curd
Zest and juice of 1 lemon
Sugar to taste

METHOD

Beat egg yolks with half the sugar till light and fluffy. Sift in cornflour, add zest and juice of lemon. Stir in fromage frais. In separate bowl whisk egg whites till stiff. Whisk in remaining sugar. Lightly fold egg whites into fromage frais mixture. Spoon mixture into 8 buttered ramekins. Run knife around edges to make rise inwards, not outwards. Place in bain-marie (roasting tin half filled with hot water) and bake for 15-20 minutes at 350°F/180°C/Gas 4 till firm. Leave to cool in fridge for at least 6 hours. Remove soufflés from ramekins and place individually on ear-dishes. Whisk ingredients for lemon sauce together and pour around soufflés. Bake at 400°F/200°C/Gas 6 for about 10 minutes. Serve with a dusting of icing sugar.

serves 6

UPSIDE DOWN PEAR & GINGERBREAD PUDDING SERVED WITH TOFFEE SAUCE

An idea of my elder son, Guy, who is my best critic!

INGREDIENTS

4 ozs (100g) butter
4 ozs (100g) soft brown sugar
15 ozs (415g) tin of pears in fruit juice
4 ozs (100g) plain flour
Half teaspoon bicarbonate of soda
2 teaspoons cinnamon
1 teaspoon ground ginger
Pinch nutmeg and cloves
1 egg, lightly beaten
4 ozs (100g) dark brown sugar
3 ozs (75g) treacle
¼ pt (150ml) milk
Double cream for serving

Fudge Sauce:
4 ozs (100g) butter
6 ozs (150g) soft brown sugar
½ pt (300ml) double cream
Few drops vanilla essence

METHOD

Make topping first by melting 2 ozs (50g) butter and soft brown sugar. Stir for 1-2 minutes over gentle heat. Pour into ovenproof dish 8" (20cm) diameter. Arrange sliced pears in fan shape over sauce. Sieve together into bowl the flour, bicarbonate of soda, cinnamon, ginger, cloves and nutmeg. Melt remaining butter and mix in egg, dark brown sugar, treacle and milk. Stir into dry ingredients and mix well. Spoon mixture over pears. Smooth surface and bake at 350°F/180°C/Gas 4 for 40-50 minutes. Remove from oven, leave to settle for 2 minutes and then turn out onto warm plate. Serve with hot fudge sauce and cream.

Hot Fudge Sauce:
Place butter, sugar and cream in saucepan and heat gently till butter is melted and sugar dissolved. Simmer sauce for 3-5 minutes and add few drops vanilla essence.

serves 6

CHOCOLATE & PEAR FLAN

Pears and chocolate go together so well.

INGREDIENTS

Pastry:
4 ozs (100g) butter
6 ozs (150g) plain flour
1 teaspoon icing sugar

Filling:
6 tinned or freshly-cooked pears
8 ozs (225g) Bournville chocolate
1 oz (25g) plain flour
4 ozs (100g) butter, softened
3 eggs
4 ozs (100g) ground almonds (leave a little for dusting top)
Crème fraîche for decoration

METHOD

Whizz pastry ingredients in processor till like fine breadcrumbs. Mould into 7” (17.5 cm) flan dish. Cool in fridge. Place on hot tray and bake at 350°F/180°C/Gas 4 for 20-25 minutes. Cool. Break chocolate into pieces and melt with butter in bowl over hot water. Whisk eggs well, fold in flour and ground almonds. Beat in the chocolate. Spoon half mixture into flan. Halve pears and arrange on top. Spoon over rest of chocolate mixture and sprinkle top with ground almonds. Bake at 300°F/150°C/Gas 2 for about 45 minutes. Serve with blob of crème fraîche.

serves 6

MINI BAKED ALASKAS WITH WARM CHOCOLATE SAUCE

A real cheat that looks sensational!

INGREDIENTS

1 small Madeira/sponge cake
1 tub best chocolate ice-cream
3 egg whites
6 ozs (150g) caster sugar
6 strawberries (for decoration)

Chocolate Sauce:
6 ozs (150g) plain Bournville chocolate
6 tablespoons single cream

METHOD

Make sauce first by gently heating chocolate and cream together till melted. Beat well till smooth and glossy. Keep warm. Cut 3"- 4" (7.5-10cm) rounds of Madeira/sponge cake with pastry cutter. Whisk egg whites till very stiff. Add caster sugar slowly. Place in piping bag. Place rounds of cake individually onto ovenproof ear dish/plate. Scoop ice-cream on top. Pipe meringue mixture around and over the top. Bake at 400°F/200°C/Gas 6 for 8-10 minutes till slightly brown. Serve immediately surrounded by warm chocolate sauce and decorated with a strawberry.

serves 6

SLICED NECTARINES WITH FUDGE SAUCE

Truly yummy.

INGREDIENTS

6 large, good, halved and stoned nectarines
½ pt (300ml) double cream
4 ozs (100g) butter
6 ozs (150g) soft brown sugar
1 lb (450g) raspberries or strawberries

METHOD

Place sliced nectarines, fanned out, onto dessert plate and decorate with mint leaf and raspberries. Place butter, sugar and cream in pan. Melt over gentle heat till sugar is dissolved, then boil for 5 minutes. Cool slightly and serve on side of plate with nectarines.

ICED CHOCOLATE & LEMON TERRINE WITH HOT CHOCOLATE SAUCE

Wickedly wonderful - happiness is an elasticated waist!

INGREDIENTS

1 pt (600ml) double cream
1 large tin Nestlé condensed milk
Rind and juice of 3 lemons
1 tablespoon Grand Marnier

Chocolate Filling:
6 ozs (150g) plain Bournville chocolate
6 tablespoons single cream

Chocolate Sauce:
6 ozs (150g) Bournville chocolate
6 tablespoons single cream

METHOD

Whip double cream and Nestlé milk till thickens. Add 1 tablespoon Grand Marnier (optional) and juice and rind of 3 lemons. Place half of ice-cream mixture into terrine mould and place in freezer. Meanwhile, make chocolate filling by melting chocolate and single cream together over low heat. Cool a little. After 20 minutes take terrine out of freezer. Pour over chocolate filling then freeze for further 20-30 minutes till starting to set. Take out of freezer and spread other half of ice-cream evenly over top. Cover with cling-film and freeze for 3-4 hours. To serve, turn out (it may be necessary to dip base of tin in warm water) onto flat glass plate. Decorate with grated chocolate. Slice as a terrine and serve with warm chocolate sauce, made by heating the ingredients together, beating well, until smooth and glossy.

serves 8

ROSE BAVAROIS WITH FRESH RASPBERRIES

Creamy, light and nourishing.

INGREDIENTS

6 egg yolks
1 pt (600ml) milk
4 teaspoons powdered gelatine (dissolved in 3 tablespoons hot water)
4 ozs (100g) caster sugar
1 tablespoon cornflour
¾ pt (450ml) single cream
10 red rose petals + extra for decoration
1-2 tablespoons rose water
½ pt (300ml) double cream
8 ozs (225g) fresh raspberries

METHOD

Beat egg yolks with sugar, cornflour and a little milk. Place rest of milk and single cream in pan and bring to the boil. Pour over egg yolk mixture, whisking constantly, then return to pan. Cook gently till thickened – do not boil. Strain custard into large bowl and stir in gelatine. Set bowl over iced water to cool mixture. Stir occasionally till beginning to set. Chop the rose petals finely and stir into cooked mixture with the rose water. Lightly whip double cream and fold into rose bavarois. Turn into shallow soufflé dish and chill for several hours. Unmould, decorate around the edge with fresh raspberries and sprinkle with extra red rose petals.

the rose of Ballindalloch bred for us by Alec Cocker to commemorate the Castle's 450th anniversary.

The Rose looks fair but fairer we it deem
For that sweet odour which doth in it live.
The canker blooms have full as deep a dye
As the perfumed tincture of the roses,
Hang on such thorns, . . .
Die to themselves. Sweet Roses do not so:
Of their sweet deaths are sweetest odours made.

SONNET 54, WILLIAM SHAKESPEARE, 1564 - 1616

MAKE YOUR OWN POT-POURRI

You should dead head your roses so why not kill two birds with one stone by making pot-pourri. The only tip is to pick the flowers after the dew has gone, on a dry sunny morning, but before the heat of the day has begun to sap the essential oils that carry the fragrance.

Scatter the flower heads and petals on a newspaper or in a box in a dry, warm, airy attic and leave for a month or two. Then combine your rose petals in a large covered container with many different dried flowers to give a variety of smell, shape and colour, making your own personal mixture. Sprinkle with orris-root powder (to fix the scent) and as many drops of rose or lavender oil as wished. Seal tightly and leave in a warm dark place for 6 weeks, shaking occasionally. Arrange in pretty jars or containers but best of all place in lovely round flat bowls, decorated on top with scattered dried flower heads, for your guests to enjoy.

serves 4-6

CARAMELISED PASSION FRUIT & FRESH ORANGE TART

A dream, and worth every mouth-watering calorie!

INGREDIENTS

Pastry:
4 ozs (100g) butter
6 ozs (150g) plain flour
1 teaspoon icing sugar

Filling:
6 ripe passion fruit
12 fl ozs (300ml) fresh orange juice
9 ozs (250g) caster sugar
7 fl ozs (180ml) double cream
6 eggs
1 oz (25g) good dark chocolate for lining pastry
3 oranges and 3 kiwis for decoration
Icing sugar for dusting top

METHOD

Whizz pastry ingredients in processor till like fine breadcrumbs. Mould into 7" (17.5cm) flan dish. Cool in fridge. Place on hot tray and bake at 350°F/180°C/Gas 4 for 20-25 minutes. Meanwhile, melt the chocolate in Pyrex bowl over pan of simmering water. Cool a little. When pastry is cooked, brush chocolate all over inside. Cool.

For filling, halve the passion fruit and scoop pulp into pan. Pour in fresh orange juice. Boil for 10 minutes to reduce by half then rub through a sieve into a large bowl. Cool a little. Beat fruit juice with sugar, cream and eggs until smooth. Strain through sieve and pour into cooked flan case. Bake at 325°F/170°C/Gas 3 for about 35-40 minutes till set but still wobbly. Cool and chill for 2 hours. To caramelise, dust evenly with sieved icing sugar and blowtorch till a golden brown.

ICED RASPBERRY SOUFFLÉ WITH A STRAWBERRY COULIS

One of my great weaknesses!

INGREDIENTS

2 egg yolks
3 ozs (75g) caster sugar
¾ pt (450ml) double cream
1 oz (25g) oatmeal (toasted under grill)
10 ozs (275g) raspberries

Strawberry coulis:
8 ozs (225g) strawberries, hulled and liquidised + sugar to taste

METHOD

Whisk egg yolks with caster sugar till thick and creamy. Set aside. Whisk double cream till it forms soft peaks and fold into egg mixture. Add toasted oatmeal and raspberries (reserving a few for decoration). Spoon mixture into dariole moulds. Freeze for about 12 hours. To serve, turn soufflés out onto individual plates. Surround with raspberries and drizzle with strawberry coulis.

serves 8-10

CHOCOLATE MOUSSELINE CAKE

A superb birthday dinner cake.

INGREDIENTS

1 lb (450g) good dark chocolate
8 large eggs, separated
8 ozs (225g) sugar
1 tablespoon Drambuie
1 tablespoon warm water
1 pt (600ml) double cream and some strawberries for decoration

For Sponge Base:
2 ozs (50g) plain flour
2 eggs
2 ozs (50g) caster sugar
2 tablespoons cocoa powder
2 ozs (50g) melted butter

METHOD

Make sponge base first. Place eggs and sugar in bowl over simmering water and whisk till light and fluffy. Sieve flour and cocoa and fold into egg mixture. Pour melted butter slowly into sponge mixture, folding in gently with large spatula. Place in 10" (25cm) greased and lined spring-loaded cake tin and bake at 350°F/180°C/Gas 4 for 10-15 minutes till risen and springy to touch. Cool.

Meanwhile, break chocolate into pieces and melt in bowl over hot water. Set aside. Place egg yolks and sugar in bowl and whisk till light and fluffy. Stir in melted chocolate, then warm water and Drambuie. Whisk egg whites in bowl till like soft peaks. Stir quarter of egg whites lightly into chocolate mixture and then add the rest carefully. Pour mousse onto sponge cake and bake at 350°F/180°C/Gas 4 for 15 minutes. Take out of oven. Cool and place in fridge for at least two hours. Remove from fridge 15 minutes before serving. Cut into slices with hot, wet knife and plate surrounded by a little double cream sprinkled with chocolate and a few sliced strawberries.

teas

- SCOTTISH FAVOURITES

teas - SCOTTISH FAVOURITES

CHOCOLATE SCONES

The best scone ever!

INGREDIENTS

8 ozs (225g) sieved self-raising flour
2 ozs (50g) butter
1 tablespoon caster sugar
2 ozs (50g) chocolate chips
¼ pt (150ml) milk

METHOD

Place flour in bowl. Cut butter into small pieces and rub into flour until mixture resembles fine breadcrumbs. Stir in sugar and chocolate chips. Mix in enough milk to form soft dough. Roll out dough on lightly floured surface till about 1" (2.5cm) thick. Cut into rounds and place onto lightly greased baking tray. Brush with a little milk and bake at 425°F/220°C/Gas 7 for 10-12 minutes till risen and golden brown. Serve split and spread with whipped cream and chocolate spread.

Mrs Betty Cameron - treasured family cook

CARROT & BANANA CAKE

Lovely and moist, with a strong taste of banana.

INGREDIENTS

6 ozs (175g) soft light brown sugar
10 ozs (275g) plain flour
1½ teaspoons baking powder
6 ozs (150g) carrots – washed and grated
3 medium eggs, lightly beaten
6 fl ozs (175ml) sunflower oil
2 medium bananas, mashed

Icing:
8 ozs (225g) low fat soft cheese
4 tablespoons icing sugar
1 teaspoon vanilla essence

METHOD

Sift together flour and baking powder. Stir in brown sugar, bananas, carrots, eggs and oil. Mix well and pour into 7" (17.5cm) greased and lined cake tin. Bake for 45-50 minutes at 350°F/180°C/Gas 4, until well risen. Cool. Beat all icing ingredients together till smooth. Cover cake with icing and decorate.

CHOCOLATE CHIP FLAPJACK

A new look to the old favourite!

INGREDIENTS

5 ozs (125g) butter
3 ozs (75g) caster sugar
1 tablespoon golden syrup
12 ozs (350g) rolled oats
3 ozs (75g) dark chocolate chips
2 ozs (50g) sultanas

METHOD

Place butter, caster sugar and golden syrup in pan and melt till mixed. Remove from heat, stir in rolled oats and mix well. Add chocolate chips and sultanas, and mix well. Turn into 8" (20cm) greased square shallow cake tin. Bake for 30 minutes in oven at 350°F/180°C/Gas 4. Cool slightly and mark into squares. When almost cold cut into squares and transfer to wire rack till cold.

Family dinner service by Ridgeway, 1820

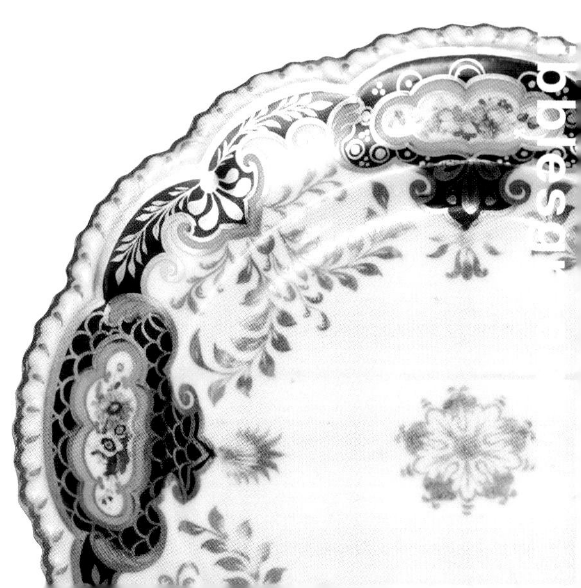

CHOCOLATE CHUNK SHORTBREAD

A really superb shortbread.

INGREDIENTS

10 ozs (275g) unsalted butter, softened
6 ozs (150g) golden caster sugar
3 ozs (75g) Bournville chocolate, chopped into chunks
3 ozs (75g) Cadbury's milk chocolate, chopped into chunks
8 ozs (225g) sifted plain flour
4 ozs (100g) semolina
Pinch of salt

METHOD

Place softened butter and sugar in bowl. Beat together until light and fluffy. Add chocolate chunks, flour, semolina and salt. Stir gently with wooden spoon until crumbly. Do not over-beat or the shortbread will be tough. Transfer the mixture into a buttered 9" x 13" (23cm x 33cm) Swiss roll tin. Press into tin evenly and prick lightly all over with a fork. Bake at 300°F/150°C/Gas 2 for about 40 minutes, until golden brown. Remove from oven and cut into squares or fingers. Leave in tin to cool then place on a wire rack.

COFFEE WALNUT CAKE

Oliver's favourite!

INGREDIENTS

8 ozs (225g) self-raising flour
1 teaspoon baking powder
8 ozs (225g) caster sugar
8 ozs (225g) softened butter
4 eggs
4 ozs (100g) chopped walnuts
1 tablespoon strong instant coffee dissolved in 1 tablespoon boiling water

Coffee Icing:
6 ozs (150g) soft butter
4 ozs (100g) sifted icing sugar
1 tablespoon of coffee (made as above)
10 walnut halves to decorate

METHOD

Place all cake ingredients (except chopped walnuts) in processor and whizz till thoroughly mixed. Add drop of milk to give right consistency. Fold in walnuts and mix well. Pour into 2 greased 8" (20cm) cake tins and bake at 350°F/180°C/Gas 4 for about 30 minutes, till firm to the touch. Cool and turn onto wire rack. Meanwhile, make coffee icing. Place all ingredients in processor and whizz till creamy. Sandwich the cakes together with coffee icing, leaving some for the top. Decorate with halved walnuts.

comfort eating ...

"NO NEED FOR ANOTHER CHOCOLATE CAKE!"

The chocolate cake to die for!

INGREDIENTS

8 ozs (225g) self-raising flour
5 eggs, beaten
10 ozs (275g) butter
10 ozs (275g) caster sugar
1 teaspoon baking powder (sieved)
2 ozs (50g) cocoa powder (sieved)
1-2 tablespoons milk
1 pkt of plain chocolate drops

Chocolate Icing:
6 ozs (175g) good dark chocolate
8 ozs (225g) butter
2 ozs (50g) cocoa powder (sifted)
10 ozs (275g) icing sugar (sifted)

METHOD

Place all ingredients, except milk and chocolate drops, into mixer and whizz for about 10 seconds. Add tablespoon or two of milk to make runny consistency. Fold in chocolate drops and pour into 2 x 9" (23cm) round non-stick greased and lined sandwich tins. Bake for 25-35 minutes at 350°F/180°C/Gas 4. Cool in tin for 10 minutes. Then turn out onto wire rack. Cool. Place all chocolate icing ingredients in pan and melt slowly. Beat well till glossy. Sandwich cake together with chocolate icing, leaving enough for top and sides.

ORANGE SCONES

A great treat for breakfast served with home-made marmalade.

INGREDIENTS

8 ozs (225g) sieved self-raising flour
1½ teaspoons baking powder
1oz (25g) soft brown sugar
Pinch of salt
2 ozs (50g) butter
Grated zest of 1 orange
2 ozs (50g) raisins
5 ozs (125ml) plain or orange yogurt

METHOD

Mix flour, sugar and salt with baking powder and rub in butter. Add raisins, orange zest and yogurt. Mix to a dough. Knead briefly and pat out to 1" (2.5cm) thick. Cut into rounds with pastry cutter. Place rounds on greased and floured baking tray and bake at 400°F/200°C/Gas 6 for 10-12 minutes till risen and golden.

ICED APRICOT TRAY BAKE

Tastes even better than it looks.

INGREDIENTS

1 cup finely chopped dried apricots
5 ozs (125g) butter
2 teaspoons grated orange rind
4 ozs (100g) brown sugar
2 eggs
1 tablespoon orange juice
8 ozs (225g) self-raising flour

Orange Icing:
4 ozs (100g) icing sugar
½ oz (15g) butter, softened
2 teaspoons grated orange rind
1 tablespoon orange juice
2 ozs (50g) chopped walnuts

METHOD

Soak apricots in boiling water for about 10 minutes till soft. Drain well. Cream butter, rind and sugar in small bowl with electric mixer till light and fluffy. Beat in eggs, one at a time. Stir in orange juice and apricots, then sifted flour. Spread mixture into greased 10" x 12" (25cm x 30cm) Swiss roll tin. Bake in oven at 350°F/180°C/Gas 4 for about 20 minutes. Meanwhile, make orange icing. Sift icing sugar into small heatproof bowl, add softened butter, orange juice and rind to make a stiff paste. Stir over hot water till icing is spreadable. Spread apricot cake with icing and sprinkle with walnuts. Cool in tin before cutting.

MRS D'S SCOTTISH BROWN BREAD

A wonderfully quick recipe, given to me by our dear family friend, Mrs Douglas, who lived on the Estate for over 50 years.

INGREDIENTS

4 ozs (100g) self-raising flour
8 ozs (225g) wholemeal flour or granary flour
1 small teaspoon bicarbonate of soda
1 small teaspoon cream of tartar
1 small teaspoon sugar
½ pt (300ml) milk
A pinch of salt

METHOD

Mix dry ingredients together. Add milk and mix well. Pour into loaf tin, cover with foil and bake at 375°F/190°C/Gas 5 for 35 minutes. Remove foil and bake for further 5 minutes.

TIP – delicious if you add 3 ozs (75g) chopped walnuts or pecans or almonds.

Rob Roy
McGregor

In our archives is a rare letter signed by Rob Roy McGregor - the famous outlaw - regarding safe passage of Colonel William Grant's cattle

naughties

- MIDNIGHT FEASTS & 'MUSTS' FOR THE KITCHEN TEA TIN

naughties - MIDNIGHT FEASTS & 'MUSTS' FOR THE KITCHEN TEA TIN

BLUEBELLE'S BROWNIES

So called as my delicious blue roan spaniel ate a tray! Quite the best brownie recipe ever – you have to make them.

naughties

INGREDIENTS

7 ozs (200g) low fat soft cheese
2 eggs
9 ozs (250g) caster sugar
½ teaspoon vanilla essence
4 ozs (100g) butter
3 tablespoons cocoa powder
4 ozs (100g) self-raising flour (sifted)
2 ozs (50g) pecans, chopped

Fudge Icing:
2 ozs (50g) butter
1 tablespoon milk
4 ozs (100g) icing sugar
2 tablespoons cocoa powder

METHOD

Beat together cheese, vanilla and 1 oz (25g) of caster sugar till smooth. Beat eggs and remaining caster sugar until light and fluffy. Place butter and cocoa in pan and heat gently until mixture is melted. Then stir into egg mixture. Fold in flour and nuts. Pour half of brownie mixture into lightly greased 8" (20cm) square shallow cake tin with parchment lining on base. Level and carefully spread the cheese mixture over it. Then cover with rest of mixture. Bake for 40-45 minutes in oven at 350°F/180°C/Gas 4. Cool in tin. Meanwhile, make icing by melting butter in milk. Stir in icing sugar and cocoa powder and mix well. Spread icing over brownies and decorate with pecan nuts. Leave icing to set, then cut into squares.

BALLINDALLOCH CHOCOLATE CRUNCH

Good for midnight feasts and a must for children of all ages - especially husbands!

INGREDIENTS

8 ozs (225g) digestive biscuits (magimixed or bashed in plastic bag with roller if larger chunks of biscuit preferred)
4 ozs (100g) butter
3 large tablespoons golden syrup
2 ozs (50g) drinking chocolate
6-8 ozs (175-225g) cooking chocolate

METHOD

Line a small Swiss roll tin with cling film. Melt butter and syrup, add drinking chocolate and biscuits. Pour into tin and flatten. Cool. Melt cooking chocolate in a bowl over boiling water and spread evenly over mixture. Cool. Pull out crunch. Take off cling film and cut into squares.

BALLINDALLOCH SHORTBREAD

A must in every Scottish household.

INGREDIENTS

8 ozs (225g) plain flour
4 ozs (100g) cornflour
4 ozs (100g) icing sugar
8 ozs (225g) butter

The library

METHOD

Chop butter into small pieces and place into processor with sieved flour, cornflour and icing sugar. Whizz until it gathers into a ball. Turn out onto floured surface and roll out to ½ inch thick. Cut into rounds with pastry cutter and place on greased baking tray. Cook for 15-20 minutes at 350°F/180°C/Gas 4 till firm and light brown. Place on wire rack and sprinkle with caster sugar while warm.

TIP – To keep shortbread fresh and crisp place in plastic bag when cool, and then place in an airtight tin.

CARROT & GINGER CAKE

Extraordinary and delicious textures.

INGREDIENTS

8 ozs (225g) plain flour
1 teaspoon baking powder
1 teaspoon bicarbonate of soda
2 teaspoons ground ginger
½ teaspoon salt
6 ozs (175g) light muscovado sugar
8 ozs (225g) grated carrots
2 pieces stem ginger in syrup – chopped
Fresh ginger, chopped
2 ozs (50g) seedless raisins
2 medium eggs, beaten
3 tablespoons corn oil
Juice of 1 orange

Icing:
8 ozs (225g) low fat soft cheese
4 tablespoons icing sugar
1 teaspoon vanilla essence

METHOD

Sift flour, baking powder, bicarbonate of soda, ground ginger and salt into bowl. Stir in sugar, carrots, chopped stem ginger, chopped fresh ginger and raisins. Beat together eggs, oil and orange juice, and pour into mixture. Spoon mixture into 8-inch (20cms) round cake tin lined with baking parchment. Bake in oven for 1-1¼ hours at 350°F/180°C/Gas 4, or until a skewer inserted into centre of cake comes out clean. Make icing while cake is cooling. Place soft cheese in bowl and beat to soften, add icing sugar and vanilla essence. Mix well and smooth over cake when cool.

WONDERFUL SCOTTISH TABLET (Fudge)

This is gorged by the ton.

INGREDIENTS

1½ lb (675g) granulated sugar
3 ozs (75g) butter
2 small tins of Carnation milk

METHOD

Bring sugar, milk and butter slowly to the boil, stirring occasionally. Boil for 25-30 minutes. Take off heat and beat till thick. Pour into greased tin, leave to cool for ½ hour. Cut into squares in tin and leave to cool for another 2 hours.

... just enough time to catch up on some old reading!

Catalogue of Books
Belonging to
Major William Grant of
Ballindalloch

Novr 11th 1766

CHOCOLATE HAZELNUT CAKE

A mouthwatering, nutty cake.

INGREDIENTS

9 ozs (250g) whole blanched hazelnuts
9 ozs (250g) unsalted butter
9 ozs (250g) Bournville plain chocolate
6 large eggs, separated
7 ozs (175g) golden caster sugar

METHOD

Roast nuts in oven at 325°F/170°C/Gas 3 for about 15 minutes, or until slightly darkened. Place nuts in processor and whizz until like breadcrumbs. Melt butter and chocolate in pan and stir well. Cool. Beat egg yolks with sugar until thick and creamy. Beat egg whites until stiff. Fold egg yolks into chocolate mixture, then fold in ground hazelnuts. Fold in whites slowly. Pour mixture into a 9½" (24cm) buttered and lined springform cake tin and bake at 325°F/170°C/Gas 3 for about 40 minutes. Remove from oven and cool for 10 minutes, then remove the sides of tin and cool on wire rack.

FRUIT & NUT MILLIONAIRE'S SHORTBREAD

Oh dear!

INGREDIENTS

Shortbread:
4 ozs (100g) butter
2 ozs (50g) caster sugar
6 ozs (150g) plain flour

Toffee:
4 ozs (100g) butter
2 ozs (50g) caster sugar
2 tablespoons golden syrup
1 tin (7 ozs) sweetened condensed milk
few drops of vanilla essence
2 tablespoons golden syrup
3 ozs (75g) raisins
3 ozs (75g) whole hazelnuts

Topping:
8 ozs (225g) Bournville chocolate

METHOD

For base:

Cream sugar and butter together, knead in flour. Press into tin 8" by 12" (20cms x 30cms). Bake at 325°F/160°C/Gas 3 for approximately 20 minutes till light brown. Leave to cool.

For toffee & topping:

Melt all toffee ingredients (not raisins or hazelnuts) in pan and boil for 5 minutes, stirring continually. Cool a little. Sprinkle raisins and hazelnuts over shortbread, then pour toffee over. Cool. Melt chocolate in bowl over pan of boiling water, and spread on top of toffee. When set and cool, cut into squares.

PINEAPPLE WHISKY FRUIT CAKE

Deliciously moist, keeps well and is ideal to leave in a tin for the unexpected visitor.

INGREDIENTS

6 ozs (150g) Demerara sugar
4 ozs (100g) butter
1 tin (400g) crushed pineapple
12 ozs (350g) mixed fruit
4 ozs (100g) cherries
1 tablespoon Glenfiddich whisky
2 eggs, beaten
9 ozs (250g) self-raising flour

METHOD

Simmer first 5 ingredients in pan for a few minutes. Add 2 beaten eggs and 9 ozs (250g) self-raising flour. Mix in whisky. Bake in 2 lb bread tin for 1¼-1½ hours at 350°F/180°C/Gas 4.

nibbles

– FAVOURITE CHEESE SNACKS

red squirrels are a particular wildlife attraction at Ballindalloch

nibbles - FAVOURITE CHEESE SNACKS

CHEESE SABLÉS

They melt in the mouth and are perfect to serve with the cheese course.

INGREDIENTS

2 ozs (50g) butter
2 ozs (50g) plain flour
2 ozs (50g) cheddar cheese
½ teaspoon mustard powder
Salt and pepper
Beaten egg
A few chopped walnuts or sea salt

METHOD

Rub the butter lightly into flour till the mixture is similar to breadcrumbs. Add grated cheese, mustard powder, seasoning and blend together into dough. Roll out onto floured surface to about ¼ inch (1cm) thick, and cut into rounds or triangles. Brush with beaten egg and sprinkle with walnuts or sea salt. Bake at 375°F / 190°C / Gas 5 for about ten minutes. Place on rack to cool.

CHEESE SHORTBREAD

Very more-ish!

INGREDIENTS

8 ozs (225g) plain flour
4 ozs (100g) cornflour
4 ozs (100g) grated Parmesan cheese, plus extra for sprinkling
8 ozs (225g) butter

METHOD

Chop butter into small pieces and place in processor with sieved flour, cornflour and Parmesan. Whizz until it gathers into a ball. Turn out onto floured surface and roll out to approximately ¼ inch (1 cm) thick. Cut into rounds with pastry cutter and place on a greased baking tray. Bake at 375°F/190°C/Gas 5 for 15-20 minutes until firm and light brown. Place on wire rack and sprinkle with Parmesan.

The auld pantry

PARMESAN DROPS

Nice and light.

INGREDIENTS

3 ozs (75g) grated Parmesan
3 ozs (75g) unsalted butter
3 ozs (75g) sifted plain flour
Salt

METHOD

Place all ingredients in food processor and whizz until forming large clumps. Remove from processor and roll into a long sausage shape on sheet of cling-film. Chill in fridge for about 1 hour, then cut into 18-20 thin slices. Place onto greased baking tray and prick with a fork. Bake at 300°F/150°C/Gas 2 for about 15 minutes till pale golden brown. Cool on rack.

STILTON & WALNUT SABLÉS

Really cheesy.

INGREDIENTS

8 ozs (225g) plain flour
4 ozs (100g) butter, diced, plus extra for greasing
5 ozs (125g) Stilton
3 ozs (75g) chopped walnuts
2 egg yolks
Beaten egg to glaze
Sea salt for sprinkling

METHOD

Place butter and flour in processor and whizz until like fine breadcrumbs. Crumble in 4 ozs (100g) of Stilton cheese and 2 ozs (50g) of walnuts. Whizz briefly to mix. Add egg yolks and whizz to paste. Roll out pastry to about ¼ inch (1cm) thick on a lightly-floured pastry board, and stamp out 2" (5cm) rounds. Transfer to baking sheet and prick lightly with a fork. Brush with beaten egg. Crumble remaining cheese and sprinkle over with reserved broken walnuts. Bake at 350°F/180°C/Gas 4 for about 15-20 minutes, till just golden. Cool on wire rack.

greens

– FAVOURITE VEGETABLE RECIPES FROM BALLINDALLOCH CASTLE

'Life is a game but golf is serious'
Ballindalloch Castle Golf Course

FAVOURITE VEGETABLE RECIPES FROM BALLINDALLOCH CASTLE

The Laburnum Archway at Ballindalloch

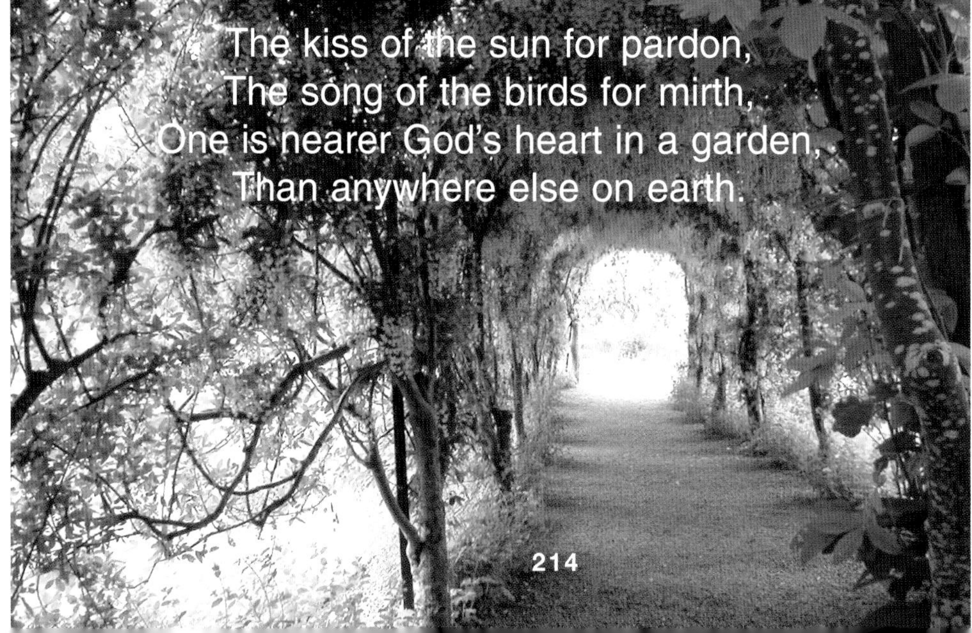

VEGETABLE DAUPHINOIS

Wonderfully easy vegetarian meal or as accompaniment to a roast.

INGREDIENTS

1 lb 2 ozs (500g) finely sliced potatoes
1 onion, finely chopped
1 parsnip, finely chopped
1 courgette, chopped
1 teaspoon chopped fresh rosemary/thyme
12 ozs (350g) sliced carrots
1 pint (600ml) single cream
Seasoning
4 ozs (100g) Parmesan cheese, freshly grated

METHOD

Layer potatoes and parsnips at bottom of ovenproof dish. Sprinkle with onions and half the rosemary. Season. Place chopped carrots on top. Pour over cream. Sprinkle Parmesan cheese over top and bake at 350°F/180°C/Gas 4 for about 1 hour till golden.

COUSCOUS

Nothing to do with Ballindalloch
but included here because
the family loves it!

INGREDIENTS

1 tablespoon sesame oil
2 teaspoons crushed coriander pods
1 teaspoon crushed cardamom
2 teaspoons ground turmeric
¾ pint (450ml) water
2 ozs (50g) sultanas
8 ozs (225g) couscous
2 ozs (50g) butter
½ teaspoon salt

METHOD

Heat the oil and spices in a medium saucepan for 2 minutes. Then add water, sultanas and salt and bring to the boil. Remove from the heat and stir in the couscous. Cover the pan and leave to stand for 10 minutes. Add the butter and cook gently for 5 minutes, stirring constantly. Remove from the heat, strain and serve.

DILL COURGETTES

Prepared imaginatively, nothing beats courgettes for flavour.

INGREDIENTS

3 tablespoons olive oil
10 ozs (275g) small courgettes, sliced lengthways into ¼" (1cm) strips
Salt and black pepper
2 tablespoons caster sugar
3 tablespoons dill vinegar or white wine vinegar
2 tablespoons chopped dill

METHOD

Heat the olive oil in a large heavy-based frying pan, then stir in the courgettes. Sprinkle the courgettes with a little salt and plenty of black pepper, then add the sugar. Turn the courgettes until they begin to brown, about 3 minutes. As soon as the courgettes begin to brown, add the vinegar and chopped dill. Continue to cook for about 2 minutes, turning the courgettes until the vinegar has evaporated. Remove from the heat and serve immediately.

HONEY MUSTARD PARSNIPS & MARMALADE BEETROOT

My son, Guy's favourite vegetables done in the most fabulous ways.

INGREDIENTS (PARSNIPS)

6-8 parsnips, peeled and quartered lengthways
2 tablespoons olive oil
2 tablespoons mustard seeds, brown or white
2 tablespoons runny honey
Seasoning

METHOD

Cut any woody parts from the centre of the parsnips and discard. In bowl, whisk together oil, mustard seeds, honey and seasoning. Put parsnips in roasting tin, drizzle over the oil and toss together. Cook for 40-50 minutes in moderate oven till golden.

INGREDIENTS (BEETROOT)

12 ozs (350g) cooked fresh beetroot
2 teaspoons red wine vinegar
3 tablespoons Seville orange marmalade
Grated rind and juice of 1 small orange

METHOD

Place the beetroot chunks in pan together with vinegar, marmalade, orange rind and juice. Cook over a moderate heat for 5 minutes, until the marmalade has melted and the ingredients are piping hot. Serve immediately.

SAUTÉED BROCCOLI

Healthy and filling.

INGREDIENTS

1 lb (450g) broccoli, divided into florets
Salt
2 tablespoons cashew nuts
1 teaspoon butter

METHOD

Cut the broccoli stems into bite-sized pieces. Discard any tough stringy stems. Fill a medium-sized pan three-quarters full with water, add a little salt and bring to the boil. Add the broccoli stems and boil gently for 2 minutes, then add the broccoli florets and cook for a further 2 minutes. Drain well. Place in ovenproof dish. Dot butter on top and sprinkle with cashew nuts.

Before the 18th century artist Thomas Gainsborough concentrated on Society portraiture, he produced some of the most sublime views of the British countryside in his landscape paintings. The positioning of trees within his pictures was achieved by him and his children arranging broccoli on the kitchen table.

the castle garden

POTATO DAUPHINOIS

The old favourite – beats mash any day!

INGREDIENTS

2½ lbs (1kg) potatoes (Desirée), peeled and sliced
2 onions
2 ozs (50g) butter
1 pt (600ml) single cream
3 ozs (75g) grated Cheddar cheese
1 oz (25g) Parmesan, grated
2 sprigs rosemary, chopped
Salt and pepper to taste

METHOD

Arrange layer of sliced potatoes over base of buttered ovenproof dish. Sprinkle with half the grated onion, rosemary and grated Cheddar cheese. Season. Add another layer of potatoes, sprinkle with rest of onion, rosemary and grated Cheddar. Season. Add last layer of potatoes and sprinkle with Parmesan. Pour cream over top and bake in oven at 350°F/180°C/Gas 4 for about an hour, till crisp and golden.

PURÉED PARSNIPS

A twist on the favourite vegetable.

INGREDIENTS

1½ lbs (675g) parsnips, peeled and chopped
Salt
¼ pt (150ml) single cream
1 oz (30g) butter
1 tablespoon horseradish sauce
1 tablespoon chopped parsley to garnish

METHOD

Cook the parsnips in pan of boiling salted water until they are soft - about 10 minutes. Drain the parsnips well in colander, then return to pan and stir in cream, butter and horseradish sauce. Mash parsnips over low heat until they are creamy and smooth. Serve sprinkled with the chopped parsley.

ROSTI

Great texture and taste.

INGREDIENTS

1 lb (450g) potatoes (Desirée is a good variety)
2 tablespoons butter
1 tablespoon sunflower oil
Flat-leaved parsley sprig to garnish
Seasoning

METHOD

Grate potatoes coarsely then rinse under running water for 1 minute, tossing all the time. Squeeze as dry as possible in tea-towel, then turn into bowl. Sprinkle with salt and pepper and form mixture into rounds about 3" (7cm) in diameter. Heat butter and sunflower oil in large heavy-based frying pan. Fry the potato rounds, in batches, over a gentle heat for 6 minutes on each side till golden brown. Drain on paper towels and serve immediately, garnished with a sprig of flat-leaved parsley.

wash under running water

SPINACH GRATIN

The best concoction by far with this vegetable.

INGREDIENTS

1 bag frozen chopped spinach
1 onion, chopped
1 oz (25g) butter
1 tablespoon flour
½ pint (300ml) milk
Seasoning
Worcestershire sauce
1 teaspoon wholegrain mustard
4 ozs (100g) Cheddar cheese, grated

METHOD

Cook spinach in teaspoon of water for few minutes. Squeeze out excess water. Melt butter, add chopped onion and cook for few minutes. Add flour to form paste. Gradually add milk and cook till sauce has thickened. Season with salt, pepper, mustard and dash of Worcestershire sauce. Add spinach to sauce and mix well. Place in gratin dish and sprinkle with grated Cheddar cheese. Bake in oven at 350°F/180°C/Gas 4 till bubbling and golden brown.

SPINACH WITH WALNUTS & LEMON

Simple but sophisticated!

INGREDIENTS

1 lb (450g) spinach
2 ozs (50g) butter
2 tablespoons walnut oil
1 garlic clove, chopped
4 ozs (100g) walnut halves
Grated rind and juice of 2 lemons

METHOD

Remove the stalks from the spinach, wash it and wring it out. Heat the butter and oil in a large frying pan with the garlic and walnuts. Cook until the garlic begins to turn golden and the nuts are just toasted. Add the spinach, lemon juice and lemon rind to the pan. Cook the spinach over a fast heat for 2 minutes, turning all the time. Remove from the heat and keep warm until ready to serve.

woof!

Mummy 'Bluebelle' and 'her five' at the Ballindalloch Milk Bar - June 2004

woof! - ... LET'S NOT FORGET THE DOG!

My favourite hobby, training - or trying to train - my dogs!

DOGGIE CHOCOLATE CRUNCH

To be eaten in **small** amounts – not gobbled!

INGREDIENTS

8 ozs (225g) dry dog food
4 ozs (100g) butter
2 ozs (50g) syrup
5 digestive biscuits, crushed

For Topping:
8 ozs (225g) doggie chocolate, melted

Rose

METHOD

Melt butter and syrup together in microwave then add dry ingredients and mix together. Tip mixture into baking tray and spread out. When cool, spread melted chocolate over top. Cut into squares when set.

THE HONEY BONE

The perfect bone for the dog with a sweet tooth.

INGREDIENTS

1 cup whole wheat flour
½ cup bran
½ cup brewer's yeast
¼ cup wheatgerm
2 tablespoons honey
2 tablespoons molasses
2 tablespoons corn oil
1 egg
⅓ cup milk

"And this is my husband!"

METHOD

In large bowl combine dry ingredients. In separate bowl mix well honey, molasses, oil, egg and milk. Gradually add mixture to dry ingredients to form dough. Roll dough out to ¼ inch (1cm) thickness and cut into bone shapes. Bake at 350°F/180°C/Gas 4 on baking tray for about 15-20 minutes, till brown.

THE CHEESEY BONE

For the dog with savoury tastes.

INGREDIENTS

2 ozs (50g) margarine
6ozs (150g) grated cheddar cheese
6 ozs (150g) whole wheat flour
1 oz (25g) milk

METHOD

Cream together cheese and margarine. Add flour and milk. Mix into ball and roll out to ¼ inch (1cm) thick. Cut into bone shapes. Bake at 375°F/190°C/Gas 5 for 20 minutes, until slightly brown.

My favourite flowers -

Rose
Poppy
Bluebelle
Jasmine

woof!

O God, grant me the serenity to
accept what I cannot change, the
courage to change what I can,
and the wisdom to know the difference.

May the road rise with you
May the wind be always at your back
May the sun shine warm upon your face
And the rain fall soft upon your fields
And until we meet again
May God keep you in the hollow of his hand

WEIGHTS AND MEASURES

- but the scales always lie!

SPOON MEASUREMENTS	
1 teaspoon	5 mls
4 teaspoons	approximately 1 tablespoon
1 tablespoon	approximately 20 mls
1 rounded spoon	2 level spoons

OVEN TEMPERATURE CHART		
°C	°F	Gas Mark
110	225	¼
130	250	½
140	275	1
150	300	2
170	325	3
180	350	4
190	375	5
200	400	6
220	425	7
230	450	8
240	475	9

METRIC CONVERSION SCALE

LIQUID			SOLID		
Imperial	Exact Conversion	Recommended ml	Imperial	Exact Conversion	Recommended gm
¼ pint	142 ml	150 ml	1 oz	28.35 gm	25gm
½ pint	284 ml	300 ml	2 oz	56.7 gm	50 gm
1 pint	568 ml	600 ml	4 oz	113.4 gm	100gm
1½ pints	851 ml	900 ml	8 oz	226.8 gm	225 gm
1¾ pints	992 ml	1 litre	12 oz	340.2 gm	350 gm
			14 oz	397.0 gm	400gm
			16 oz (1 lb)	453.6 gm	450 gm
			2.2lb	1 kilogram(kg)	

AMERICAN CONVERSION OF WEIGHTS AND MEASURES

(Note: UK ounces and metric grams are weighed)

	US	Standard UK	Metric
Flour	¼ cup	1 oz	25 g
	½ cup	2 oz	50 g
	¾ cup	3 oz	75 g
	1 cup	4 oz	100 g
Icing Sugar/Cocoa/Cornflour	1 cup	4½ oz	120 g
Butter/Sugar	2 tbsp	1 oz	25 g
(caster, granulated or brown, firmly packed)	¼ cup	2 oz	50 g
	½ cup	4 oz	100 g
	¾ cup	6 oz	175 g
	1 cup	8 oz	225 g
Liquids/Cream/Yogurt	¼ cup	2.5 fl oz	60 ml
	½ cup	5 fl oz	120 ml
	¾ cup	7.5 fl oz	180 ml
	1 cup	10 fl oz	240 ml
	1 pt (2 cups)	20 fl oz	480 ml
Grated Cheese/Chopped Nuts	1 cup	4 oz	100 g
Yeast	1 cake, pkg	4 oz fresh	15 g
Rice	1 cup	8 oz	230 g

FOOD	Level spoons to 1 oz (25 g) (approximate equivalents)
Flour, cornflour and other starch powders	2 tablespoons
Fresh breadcrumbs and cake crumbs	4 tablespoons
Rolled oats	3 tablespoons
Rice	2 tablespoons
Sugar	2 tablespoons
Sultanas, seedless raisins, currants	2 tablespoons
Butter	2 tablespoons
Gelatine	3 tablespoons
Syrup, treacle, honey	1 tablespoon

INDEX

Designed and edited by Nick McCann

Recipe photographs by Simon Walton

Additional photographs by
Tony Gorzkowski, Mark Hamblin, Nick McCann, John Pickering

Dog models - Poppy, Rose, Bluebelle and Jasmine

The recipes – Haggis tartlets with red onion marmalade and whisky sauce; Smoked haddock soufflés and creamy herb sauce; Fillet of venison with oat and herb crust; Roast salmon with goat's cheese and herbs accompanied by a cream and prawn sauce; Orange/grapefruit tart; Raspberry and Drambuie tart; Chocolate chunk shortbread; Chocolate hazelnut cake; and Parmesan drops – are published in, or based on recipes published in Sue Lawrence's Scottish Kitchen, published by Headline in 2002.

Published by Heritage House Group Ltd.
Heritage House , Lodge Lane, Derby DE1 3HE
Tel: 01332 347087 Fax: 01332 290688
email: publications@hhgroup.co.uk

BALLINDALLOCH CASTLE
Ballindalloch Banffshire AB37 9AX
Tel: 01807 500206 Fax: 01807 500210
email: enquiries@ballindallochcastle.co.uk

www.ballindallochcastle.co.uk

APPLE and BANANA CRUMBLE
ENSE ET ANIMO
CHOCOLATE and ORANGE MOUSSE
CHOCOLATE QUEEN of PUDDINGS
TOUCH NOT THE CAT BUT A GLOVE
ICED RASPBERRY SOUFFLÉ with a STRAWBERRY COULIS
PASSION FRUIT DREAMS
TWICE-BAKED CHOCOLATE SOUFFLÉ
SLICED NECTARINES with FUDGE SAUCE
CHOCOLATE ICE-CREAM
TOFFEE ICE-CREAM
BLACKBERRY/RASPBERRY & APPLE SOUFFLÉ
RASPBERRY & DRAMBUIE TART
ORANGE/GRAPEFRUIT TART
ORANGE CRÈME CARAMEL
ROSE BAVAROIS with FRESH RASPBERRIES
MINI BAKED ALASKAS with WARM CHOCOLATE SAUCE
CARAMELISED PASSION FRUIT and FRESH ORANGE TART
CHOCOLATE & PEAR FLAN

AVOCADOS and SCALLOPS
GOAT'S CHEESE and THYME SOUFFLÉS
EGGS BALLINDALLOCH
FIGS, PARMA HAM and ROCKET with PARMESAN
ROQUEFORT TART
SMOKED HADDOCK MOUSSELINES with a PRAWN & HOLLANDAISE SAUCE
CRISPY PARMA HAM with AVOCADO
NORWEGIAN CREAM
BROCCOLI and SMOKED HADDOCK SOUP
SMOKED SALMON BLINI CHEATS
HAGGIS TARTLETS with RED ONION MA
ICED WHITE CHOCOLATE TERRINE with a RASPBERRY COULIS
SMOKED HADDOCK SOUFFLÉS with a CREAMY HERB SA
SMOKED SALMON and DILL TARTLETS
ENSE ET ANIMO
TOUCH NOT THE CAT BUT A GLOVE